# The Odyssey
# of a
# Spiritual Nomad

## Garth C. Nielsen

Heather and Highlands Publishing

Heather and Highlands Publishing
Garth C. Nielsen - Author
Cover Photograph Kim Victoria Copyright
© Kim Victoria 2014 All Rights Reserved.

Cover Design- Tom Watson
ISBN(13) 978-1-58478-048-9
First Edition 2014 ©
to contact the author— odysseynomad@gmail.com

# TABLE OF CONTENTS

# DEDICATION

I would like to thank my wife, Barb Nielsen of Olowan Editing Services, (olowaneditingservices@gmail.com), and dedicate this to her for her loving and constant support.

This book is also dedicated to all of the Native Peoples who have been an essential and constant part of my life over the years, in many different places; people who have shared their life ways, their concerns, their hopes and dreams, their diligence in being true to their peoples, and, in some cases, their sacred ceremonies.

The words in this book are mine, not theirs, and I humbly ask pardon from all my friends if I have said anything here to offend them in any way.

This book is also dedicated to the Maya People of Chiapas, Mexico, who have stood up and said: "Basta!", "Enough!" and are suffering for their stand to reclaim what is rightfully theirs.
Viva Zapata

To all of you , I say Thank You!

Metakuye Oyasin, All My Relations.
Garth Nielsen, Paradise, California

# INTRODUCTION

I have been asked to write some words of introduction to this collection of essays by my friend Garth Nielsen. It is a task I am glad to undertake.

Garth and I met in 1984, very soon after he and his family arrived in Tucson, Arizona. Over the years, since that meeting, our friendship has grown and strengthened. We have traveled many miles together, both literally and figuratively, sharing many good meals together, spending time talking about problems and worries, hopes and dreams. We have worked together to achieve goals and overcome obstacles. We have shared both tears and laughter.

Garth has been a good friend. I have witnessed his involvement with and commitment to indigenous concerns, working closely with him on many projects. He has been a friend and supporter of the O'odham in Mexico for many years.

Garth is also an artist and a writer, and his talents also reflect his commitment and love for indigenous peoples. His roots are in the state of Nevada and the West. He has spent many years traveling across this land, many years attempting to learn and understand how to walk on the Red Road. His words reflect his life.

Joseph Garcia, Lieutenant Governor
Traditional O'odham Leader
O'odham in Mexico

# PREFACE

I was recently asked why I wrote this book. It didn't take me long to come up with an answer. Some time ago, I saw a video produced by PBS about the Haida, a people living on Queen Charlotte's Island, off the coast of British Columbia. In this video, the narrator, a Haida woman, made a comment which really impacted my thinking. She said that when a person has lived their life and reached an age where they can be considered to be an elder, they need to have a story to relate to the younger generations. If such a person has nothing to say, no experiences to pass on, nothing of value to share, then that person's life has not been fully lived.

I feel that I have something to say. I sincerely hope that what I have written can be taken and used by some young person. Hopefully, what has been shown to me will help someone else make sense of the world in which we all live. The celebration of 75 years of living is an important event in the life of a person. In traditional cultures, at such a time, a person has what is called a "Give Away." This is a time when gifts are shared with family and friends to commemorate this special occasion. I would like to think of this book as my give away to all of you.

Metakuye Oyasin

## CHAPTER 1

# REFLECTIONS

In Native American terms, I am an elder. To put my life into some pattern, to see where I've been, to understand what has shaped my thinking, to know who and what the major influences in my life have been – this, on a superficial level, should be a fairly simple task.

Western society has a linear concept of time. A classic example is the time line in all the history books. Indigenous peoples have a cyclical concept of time. The People of the Great Plains had the Winter Count, in which they recorded significant events in their lives. These Winter Counts were kept by specific individuals who knew how to read the mnemonic devices employed in these records. These counts were not tied to dates but to events.

The events recorded on the Winter Count often had nothing in common with incidents listed in the white man's history books. Instead, when a chief offered 50 pieces of flesh from each arm at the annual Sun Dance as a prayer for the benefit of the children, this was recorded on the Winter Count. This act of self-sacrifice was remembered and honored long into the future. When gold was discovered in 1848 at Sutter's Mill, it was not recorded in the Winter Counts. But when hoards of gold seekers streamed across Indian Country, followed by the Blue Coats, steam boats on the Missouri River, small pox epidemics and the coming of the Iron Horse, all of these, which impacted directly on The People, were recorded.

I can look back and see how my life has been altered by world events. And yet, to me, just as import, maybe even more so, are the words and actions of individual people, often unknown to all but their families and friends. These people have helped me discover and explore previously unnoticed landscapes all around me, opening a whole new world.

Here is a graphic illustration: when I was a little boy, spending the summers with my grandparents, my uncle would take me hiking in the hills. He had the unique ability to give ordinary information a sense of wonder. On an unforgettable day, up in the San Gabriel Mountains, my uncle told me he would show me something that no other human being had ever seen. This statement instantly captured my imagination. Picking up a piece of granite, he struck it with another harder stone. The granite broke in half, revealing for the first time its glittering heart. This event is part of my personal Winter Count.

I was born in 1938. The last Civil War veteran died when I was in my teens. As a young child, I can recall hearing of the death of President Roosevelt. Later, I was told of the death of millions, instantly vaporized by a nuclear warhead, their shadows etched forever into solid stone. I can recall hearing the names of places: Bataan, Okinawa, Guadalcanal, Iwo Jima. It was on Iwo Jima that Ira Hayes, a Pima Indian from Arizona, helped to raise the US flag on Mount Suribachi during the last days of the Battle for the Pacific. The photograph commemorating this event was seen around the world in newspapers and magazines.

The Battle for the Pacific could not have been won without the Dine Code Talkers. In fact, this was not a code at all, but a language that was then encoded. Ironically, the speakers of this language had been beaten for speaking it as children in Bureau of Indian Affairs boarding schools. The US Armed Forces employed Navajo (Dine) speakers to use their native tongue for communication of all top secret military information, crucial to the winning of the war.

And yet, when Native American veterans, who had valiantly served their country, came home, they returned to a life of bitterness and isolation, living in the third world, on the reservations of America. Ira Hayes, who returned to Arizona as a hero, ended his life, drunk, dead in a street gutter.

In school, I was surrounded by middle class white America. The small number of Paiute children in the Reno school system seemed shy and withdrawn, going to class almost unnoticed. It was many years

The Ancient Ones knew me as the Heart of the Mountains.

Garth Nielsen

later that I discovered that one of my class mates was a descendent of Wovoka, the Ghost Dance Messiah.

Pablo Picasso, Salvador Dali, and Ted De Grazia, .... these were artists I admired. Old values were being called into question and discarded. For me, the radically new paintings of these controversial artists spoke to my soul, creating new ways of seeing the world. Years later, in a book on Native American art, I discovered a statement which speaks to the spiritual responsibility of indigenous artists. Anglo society has a phrase, "Art for art's sake." This does not even apply for Native American artists. Their creations must touch a deep spiritual connection with all of their relations in this universe. For me, Picasso, Dali and De Grazia came close to this concept.

A Native American acquaintance of mine once said to me that the Europeans on this continent are not yet able to understand this hemisphere. They have not lived here for uncounted generations. Most of them have no concept of what it is to be related to this earth and all that is upon it. They have no knowledge of how to live in balance and harmony on Turtle Island, the Native American name for North America.

As the anger and frustration of my early years drove me into myself, I became more introverted. I tried to concentrate my thoughts on art and spirituality, triggered primarily by my father's discovery of some ancient caves in Nevada. Instinctively, I knew that there was a spiritual truth to be found in this place and in these disciplines. I felt that what had been shown to Native People since the beginning of time by the Creator of All Things was now being shown to me. It took me a while, but I began to discover myself. I realized that Turtle Island was sacred. Through this earth, the people who live upon it communicate with the Creator in a constant, reciprocal cycle.

So I've listened to the words of many teachers, and they have assisted me on my odyssey. I have tested these teachings, comparing them to Christian theology. For myself, I have found that traditional Native teachings enhance the words of Christ, bringing clarity to His teaching on how to walk in balance and harmony with all creation. I have found that it is the institutionalized doctrines and the dogma that create barriers for me. I look at Western Civilization and its rapaciousness and corrupted ideals and I see a people who excuse their actions by hiding behind their interpretations of what they believe Christ said. I believe, in my heart, that the early years of pain and searching were essential in reaching the place where I am now. Personal spiritual growth only comes through travail.

Because I have incorporated the beliefs of Native Peoples into my own private worship, many who hold to a more narrow focus have accused me of abjuring my belief in Christ. This is not so. I have had no trouble in accepting both Christ's words and Native ceremonies. They have enriched my own spiritual strength. The prayers are for the well-being of all life and are a continuous cycle of thanksgiving. An enhanced spirituality has imbued my life with a sense of sacred meaning and my private rituals have strengthened this bond. Mine is a faith in synchronism, a harmonious blending of two spiritual walks.

What do we do now? Everything under the sun has been tried. We've listened to innumerable interpretations of Christ's message. We've listened to the Hippies in the '60s and to foreign gurus like the Maharishi Mahesh Yogi and the Moonies. We continue a long, well-travelled tradition of worshipping idols. We no longer have heroes or even anti-heroes, only celebrities. Perhaps it is time to stand still and listen.

I can look back from my vantage point and see where I've been. The road fades in the distance. Small crosses, descansos, personal memorials, mark spots where foolish fantasies which I hoped would give my life meaning, now lie buried. Before me, the road winds upward into the mist, the Great Mystery.

In this book, I strive to give you brief pictures of the events of my Winter Count.

## CHAPTER 2
# THINGS OF THE SPIRIT

S pirit: that which is traditionally believed to be the vital principle or animating force within living beings; that which constitutes one's unseen, intangible being.

In 1946, a few months before my birthday, I was placed upon a life path that has continued to afford new vistas of experience on an almost daily basis. Now, many decades later, that day of intellectual and spiritual awakening stands clearly in my mind's eye.

"Daddy, where did you go?" I gasped, my heart pounding.

My father and his friend had seemed to disappear into the huge, slumping mass of tufa. Intensely curious, I leaped from the car and raced across the sand, following my father's footprints.

In the shadows of the massive stone outcropping, my father stood mesmerized. Gazing slowly about him, he looked around this enormous cave. Part of the roof had fallen in, and a shaft of bright sunlight illumined part of this room. Kneeling in the pool of light, my father picked up a fragment of finely woven basket. Then, with a stick, he stirred the surface of the talcum-fine dust. In doing so, he uncovered another object, a human tooth. Placing both the tooth and the basket fragment into my hand, he said to me,

"This was someone's home a long time ago. I'll bet little boys like you lived here once."

Rising, he took my hand and we walked to the far wall. With my finger in his hand, my father drew it over the blackened surface.

"This is where the people who lived here cooked their meals," he said to me in a hushed tone. I can remember standing there, beside my father, filled with awe and wonder. I have become convinced that there are beneficent and benevolent spirits, sent by the Creator, to guide each of us. I believe that such a spirit became a part of me and my life in that ancient place so many years ago.

Over the years, I have had many intense dreams about those caves. In these dreams, a native man is watching me, his hands clutching atl atl darts. I awake, absolutely terrified and yet the man in the dream has never made any threatening gestures. The eyes of the man in my dream are still on me and they guide me to further experiences and growth.

I believe in spirits. I also believe that, at the creation of the universe, the Creator placed these animating forces within the natural world for specific purposes.

I recall one winter day, years later, walking with my young son in an isolated area of the Carson River Canyon. No one was there but my son and I. Snow was falling lightly and the wind was rustling the naked limbs of the cottonwood trees. A barely discernible movement along the ground caught the corner of my eye. Turning quickly, I saw nothing, but I had a feeling that I was being watched. Suddenly, from among the wind-blown, snow covered stones at my feet, a black and orange box elder beetle scurried in front of me. I stopped, immobilized. Here was a paradox, a summer insect in this time of ice and bitter cold. Was it merely a fluke, a miraculously surviving beetle roused from its resting place? Or was it something else?

As one who walks on a spiritual path, I'm very open about my beliefs. I've been asked often by very sincere people, "Do you really believe in spirits? Do you really believe they can work through people?"

Culturally, there are many different definitions for spirits. For me, one of the forms which the Creator takes is energy. And since all that exists is a part of the Creator, then spirits are energy as well. We humans, along with our relations, the algae, the ground squirrels, the hummingbirds, the night blooming cereus, the amoeba, or the scorpions are only compact energy forms. Our bodies are the humble huts in which this energy lives. Energy is indestructible. The body returns to dust with death. The "us" which is energy rejoins the Creator and the energy of the universe. This universal energy includes all which has been, is now or will be. It includes all of the extinct life forms: the mastodon, the brontosaurus, the crinoid and the ramapithecine.

When energy is freed, it is drawn, magnetically, to a receptive being and a new force is manifested. It can take any form within the will of the Creator, whether they be sentient or inanimate, and are alive and full of the Creator.

Art is not eternal. Only the energy that gives it life lives on. Michelangelo's marble statues will one day turn to chalk dust. The energy of his genius will live forever, perhaps to be reborn in some person, while the Rome that he knew is a mile deep under some future ocean.

CHAPTER 3

# THE TEACHINGS
# OF THE ELDERS

I don't recall the day that I realized that the road before me was my personal odyssey. I've always been a seeker, aware that my spirituality was at the center of my being and that the Creator was guiding me onto the less travelled spiritual paths.

It was the third day of the Sun Dance at Djil Nitsaa, Big Mountain, in 1988. The whole meaning of diligence had been called into question for me since I had attended my first Sun Dance three years before.

This day, questions or doubts would be eliminated entirely. For two days, I sent my strength to the dancers in the sacred circle, who had pledged to pierce for all of their relations. Each night, I returned to my tent to scribble some notes, grab a quick bite of food, retire to ponder the day's events, pray and fall into a fitful sleep. The drum, though in reality, silent at night, continued to throb throughout my dream time. I had been totally drawn into the Wi Wanyag Wacipi, the sacred ceremony of the Sun Dance. I had been told that there are no observers at this ceremony. The people, standing underneath the circular arbor surrounding the sacred Sun Dance Tree, who support the dancers with their prayers, are as much involved as the dancers themselves. The truth of these words was manifested in my mental, physical, emotional and spiritual fatigue.

It was now about noon on the third day. Many of the pledgers had pierced and broken free. I watched as a man was pierced through his chest. He stood and ran and pulled free. He then ran victoriously around the interior of the sacred circle. Then, instead of returning to his place in the line of dancers, he went, again, to the buffalo robe at the base of the sacred tree. The full import of what was taking place hit me hard. Even knowing that he was now being pierced for a second time did not prepare me for what I was about to witness. When the man stood, he had eagle feathers attached to the skin of his arms. There were skewers through his back. His assistants threw the rope over the fork of the Sun Dance Tree and slowly drew the pledger into the air, where he soared like an eagle. My eyes filled with tears. All I could think was: "Be strong, brother. Be strong!"

Later, I found out that this man's brother, who had also been a Sun Dancer, had been murdered by a white man earlier in the year. What I had witnessed was the fulfillment of the pledges of both this man and his dead brother. In this act, he was praying for not only his family, but for the killer and his family and for all of their relations.

A person's spiritual strength is fortified by their repeated participation in sacred ceremonies. It is in the repeated participation that we learn to stand before the Essence of Existence, the Great Mystery. Only in sacrifice of one kind or another is our spiritual identity allowed to take form and to grow.

Over the years, in attending Sun Dance ceremonies at Big Mountain, I've had the chance to sit down with Lakota and Dine elders. They have been willing to share their wisdom with me and I have learned much from them.

On an afternoon with the dancers resting in the ramada after one of the longest rounds of the day, Dine elders spoke softly in microphones powered by gas generators. Their melodic speech drifted outward, slowly settling upon the land and those who listened.

I walked back to my camp for a cup of coffee and a rest. As I sat there, smoking my pipe, my thoughts were totally centered on the ceremony. The warmth of the day, coupled with a not unpleasant fatigue, caused me to doze lightly.

A slight sound to my left brought me awake. A stranger stood near our fire, a Dine elder. At this point, I was unsure as to whether he spoke any English. Rising, I extended my hand to him and poured him a cup of coffee, which he accepted. I offered him a seat.

Setting his cup of coffee on the ground, the elder took out "fixings" and rolled a cigarette. We sat comfortably, smoking in silence. After a time, pointing with pursed lips toward the Sun Dance arbor, he said in perfect English: "That's a strong ceremony, isn't it?"

"There is nothing in white society that I can think of that even comes close."

The elder chuckled, drew on his cigarette and took a swallow of coffee. Still gazing toward the arbor, he continued:

"These boys from South Dakota, man, they bring their most sacred ceremony to us Dine in Arizona. Man!"

"Is this your first Sun Dance?" I asked.

The elder seemed not to hear my question. Instead, he asked me: "You know any of the people out there in the sacred circle?"

"A few," I responded, not wishing to have him think I was trying to show off.

"We got one of our Big Mountain boys out there," he said.

I told him that I knew the man he was speaking of and that he had been in our home in Tucson.

Rising, the elder handed me his coffee cup, shook my hand and said: "Mebee I'll be back tonight. I like the coffee."

"Come for supper," I said.

"Thanks," he replied and walked off across the hills.

Later that evening, he returned to share a meal with us. After we had eaten, we spoke about the Sun Dance ceremony. He said that the leaves of the Sun Dance Tree, always a cottonwood tree, are the heart of the universe. They represent the people and the passing of the generations. As each generation ages and dies, a new one comes to take its place. In this way, the wisdom and knowledge of the ancestors is passed on. The leaves also represent the hard-won sacrifices of one generation for the benefit of those yet unborn. When we see the dancers sacrificing themselves, they are dancing for the seventh generation to come as well as for their own spiritual growth and the spiritual growth of the entire world. The Sun Dance is a time of renewal and growth and a time when all is made whole.

I never knew what this man's involvement was with the Sun Dance. I only know that he was a Dine medicine man, a singer who conducted sacred ceremonies.

One of the first lessons taught to me when I placed my feet on the

Red Road, was that what one does in this life is not for himself. If there is benefit for the individual, that benefit is of secondary importance to the benefit of helping others and for preparing for the seven generations of those yet to come. Ideally, we strive to achieve love, understanding and compassion among peoples of all colors and to change the course of catastrophic ecological policies which are destroying our earth and the life upon it. In reality, each of us has our own responsibility to seek guidance, to help and love each other, and to pray daily to the Creator. The Lakota Sun Dance teaches a wonderful way in which to end each prayer. When the prayer is completed, the one speaking ends his words with: "Metakuye Oyasin," or, "All My Relations." In this way, the prayer is never ended, but merely passed on to the next one to pray.

# CHAPTER 4
# CHIAPAS

While most of the western world was sleeping off the effects of the night before, on January 1, 1994, many of us awoke to the news that a new revolution had begun in southern Mexico. Americans watching television were shocked at the scenes of carnage in the zocalo, or town square, of the colonial town of San Cristobal de las Casas in the state of Chiapas.

Amid the piles of destroyed legal documents beneath the portico of the municipal building lay bodies of Maya Indians, most still wearing ski masks or bandanas across their faces. Graffiti spray painted upon the walls announced to the world the existence of a group calling themselves EZLN, the National Zapatista Liberation Army.

A charismatic figure emerged out of the chaos of those first few weeks of warfare, calling himself Subcommandante Marcos. El Sub seems to have risen from the ashes of some long forgotten, abandoned city state in the jungle. As the spokesman for the EZLN, he talked of bringing back all that had been taken from the Maya people. He made it plain that he was willing to sacrifice himself for his people. With a ski mask, clouds of pipe smoke, two wrist watches, bandeleros of shot gun shells across his chest, he became the rallying point for all those who stand for an end to the inhuman oppression of both the Maya in Chiapas and for all indigenous peoples of Mexico.

With this revolution, Mexico was forced to acknowledge to the world that they still have indigenous peoples in their country who are far more than exotic attractions to entice tourists. Traditional Native people in North America viewed with grief the continuation of the war of genocide against their brothers and sisters in the south. Cries were heard across the continent, cries to rally in defense against those who were being slaughtered.

On a night some weeks later, the cry for help from the south was responded to in Tucson, Arizona. It was a night pregnant with tension, excitement and hope. A parish church, the size of most cathedrals, was filled to capacity. People stood two and three deep along the walls. The Pomo Peace Caravan to Chiapas had come to Tucson to talk about their mission and to ask for support. During the evening, a delegation from the Tohono O'odham Nation made the commitment to join this caravan and I was asked to join them as a driver.

It was an intense evening. The word "hope" was on everyone's lips and in everyone's prayers. There are those who claim that having faith in God is nothing but a superstition, a waste of time. You can't see God, so why should you believe in Him? Hope is invisible, as well. Should hope for a better life in this world for all people be abandoned because it is an intangible concept? In their communiques, the Zapatistas spoke of hope for the future. Were they fools for thinking that they could help to bring change to Mexico?

Chiapas is the traditional homeland of the Maya. Here the Zinacontecos have shrines where the spirits of the ancestors of each family and lineage are present. These spirits are recognized and honored in ceremonies conducted at these shrines. In the Spanish language, the shrines are called kalvaryos. I find it interesting that the word for the place where Christ was crucified was chosen to apply to these sacred places.

Some have suggested that this name, kalvaryos, is used to indicate the death of indigenous spiritual beliefs which, according to the Christian tradition, occurred when the Maya were converted by the Spanish clergy. In actuality, Christianity is only a thin veneer over indigenous sacred beliefs which are as viable today as they were before the advent of the Spaniards in the sixteenth century.

Kalvaryos is a most appropriate name for these shrines. The image of death that this word carries with it represents the death of the

In the Spirit of Zapata

Garth  Nielsen

faint hearted, the peripherally involved. It also speaks of something more, the dualism of life and death that is present for both the Maya and for Christianity.

There is a striking relationship between the ceremonial symbolism in both ancient and contemporary Maya and Christian beliefs. It concerns itself with the cross. Symbolically, for both groups, the cross is a doorway to the spirit world, representing both life and death. As a portal, it enables a priest/holy man to die to this world so that, by transformation, he/she can converse with the spirits (ancestors) and the Creator, ensuring life and its continuance on this earth.

The life and death which the cross represents is present in the words of Marcos and the EZLN. They have said: "Basta, no mas!" "Enough! No more! We will live!" Christian and Maya images overlay each other. "I come bringing life and more abundantly." As Christ lived and died on the cross, so the Maya live and die through the cross.

During the long drive down to Chiapas, the southern-most state in Mexico, and then back to Tucson, many thoughts past through my mind. I was continually reminded that the past is very much present in this beautiful country. The spirits of the land and the people are very tangible and the ancient ones are close at hand at all times. A person needs only to open the ears of his or her heart and the land will speak with an audible voice.

As the miles passed beneath the wheels of our vehicles, I questioned myself about why we were here. I recalled the history of Mexico, seeing the millions of people moving through the long valleys, guided by their prayers. Their journeys reminded me of the Hopi migration stories. I remembered the stories of blood-letting on an unprecedented scale, which became an end unto itself, helping to usher in the demise of their last world. Hopi stories tell of the remnant of people who sought peace and harmony and were guided up through a miraculous reed or cane to this present world.

With the Hopi myths present in my mind, the impact of our mission of aide to the suffering people of the south suddenly came into focus. Were we not in this caravan helping to open the joints within another reed, another bamboo cane. Were we not helping the suffering, humble ones pass up to a new world, a place of equity and compassion, a place where hope could dwell in harmony with the people?

## CHAPTER 5
# WALKING SOFTLY ON THE EARTH

In the four corners area of the southwest, where communities are often very far apart, there are endless miles of mesas, deserts and mountains, and very few people. It is an enchanted and beautiful landscape, haunted by the ones who built the isolated pueblos which hang like swallow's nests high up in the wind-carved rock shelters. It is the land of the Hopi, the Dine and the Southern Paiute. The stark beauty is a siren song which has often lured the inexperienced hiker into winding, dead-end canyons and a slow, agonizing death. Any moisture is quickly absorbed by the unyielding earth and stone. Life is precarious here and death can come with the next breath.

In the early 60s, I lived for less than a year in Moab, Utah, in the heart of the red rock mesa country, north of Monument Valley and near the Arches National Monument. In that brief period of time, this country cast a spell upon my thinking. I can understand why so many people from all over the world come to this part of the southwest. It is a paradise for hikers, mountain bikers, rock climbers and photographers. It also calls to the contemplative spirits of those who listen.

During my residence there, three people died. On one level, their deaths were caused by their own carelessness. They lost their way and died of dehydration. The summer temperatures in this area soar to well over one hundred degrees for days at a time. I've walked the desert and the mountains all my life and I've often thought about how one can become so disoriented and confused. What thoughts go through your mind on such an occasion when life is being sucked out of you by an intense and relentless sun?

I consider myself to be an experienced desert rat. I have known, since childhood, what to wear, what to take with me and how to behave in the wilderness. But it was as an adult that I was given the ultimate tool for survival. This gift was given to me by a traditional Yoeme deer singer. Because he has given me this spiritual insight, I want to introduce him by sharing my impressions of the first deer dance I ever attended.

For the Yoeme, whom the dominant society called Yaqui, one of the most important and culturally identifiable aspects of their society is the deer dance. This ceremony has its own musicians, instruments, songs, societies and regalia, totally separate from any other Yoeme ceremony. My friend is an educator and a musician. His life has been dedicated to the deer dance and he has been blessed with great knowledge. I had, since coming to Tucson, met this man on a number of occasions. He was always present with his companion at the Lenten ceremonies at Pascua Viejo in Tucson, the original Yoeme community in the United States.

Because of my involvement over the years with Native issues and beliefs, I have been privileged to attend a number of sacred ceremonies. It was at the fiesta of the anniversary of the San Xavier Mission that I saw my first deer dance. It was an unforgettable experience.

On this night, as the sun set, a bloody, crescent moon seemed to hang precariously over the bony mountains which clawed upward to the sky. The old Spanish mission, the White Dove of the Desert, loomed spectrally in the moving shadows cast by the desert and the throng of people present. Bursting rocket stars momentarily colored faces green, blue or rose.

Behind the noise of the people, from out of the depths of an ancient myth, through the fiesta and lights of the pageantry, came the resonant sound of the drum. Hidden, as the heart beat is hidden, the drum was felt but unnoticed. The throbbing arrested thoughts and transformed them to that of man's ancient, upward, spiraling path from unicellular protoplasm to light, to understanding and wisdom.

Large log bonfires cast flickering shadows on dancing figures.

Yoeme Deer Dance

Garth Nielsen

scattered like hens in a hail storm. Almost immediately, one of them backed into a cholla and impaled himself with many tiny, stinging spines. My friend, who was very soft spoken, had to raise his voice and call these people back to him.

"This is not Chicago," he said. "We have a certain way of acting in the desert. To begin, we must ask permission of the spirits of this place before we enter."

The mid-westerners glanced at each other, suddenly unsure of themselves, and someone asked, "What do we do, now?"

My teacher then said a prayer, and told the people that he would lead and they were to follow. They had not gone more than fifteen feet when they abruptly encountered a coiled western diamond backed rattlesnake. Pointing at the snake, my friend did not have to say a word. Moments later, he helped a member of the mid-westerners to avoid a large scorpion in the path. He talked to them about the importance of entering the desert with respect. The group was now well aware of what could have happened.

Since this story was told to me, I have honored my friend and his people by following his example each time I enter the desert. I believe without question that the spirits of the desert hear and are aware of our presence among them.

My wife and I were walking beside a huge pile of naturally placed boulders, massive and several stories high on a very hot southern Arizona afternoon. We were at an archaeological site that had been partially mapped and excavated and then abandoned. We were looking at petroglyphs high up on the rock faces when we stopped to rest in the shade of overhanging rocks. As we stood talking, I noticed a small in-situ metate, which had possibly been used for grinding herbs, in a large boulder near us.

I have learned, over the years, to carry tobacco, sage and cedar with me at all times. These plants are used by Native peoples through North America when prayers are being said. I placed these plants in the shallow depression and lit them and began to say a prayer.

Anyone who lives and interacts with the natural world in the rural portions of the western United States rapidly becomes aware of the habits of the animals who live there. For instance, it is well known that coyotes seldom if ever cry in the heat of the day. They serenade their listeners at dawn, at dusk and while hunting at night. They also

The water drum drew the people from the shadows. Their smiles masked their uncertainty in confronting images from an unknown past. The drummers sat in the dust. A counter rhythm was created as a man scraped a stick over a notched ironwood rasp. In an instant, time was turned backward through the centuries.

Four dancers moved to the music, each called forward in turn by the tampaleo. A reed flute was raised to thin lips and ancient notes perched on shoulders, flying when their turn came to thread themselves into the sound of the drum. A steady but hidden voice sang the story of the deer dance. In this ceremony, the words were ancient and yet ever new with each telling.

The drum's sound welled up from the circle to wash over the watchers and flood the plaza. Fed by the fires, it curled and spread out into the night to seep back, once more, into the sandy soil which had created it. Perhaps this was the first sound to emerge from the earth, the primordial sound of being.

The intensity of this ceremony held my thoughts for months. I wanted to learn as much as could about the Yoeme. I was amazed at the beauty of their ceremonies and the openness of the people. In my search to learn more, I began attending a class in Yoeme language and culture which was being held at Pascua Viejo near the capilla or chapel.

On the first night of the class, I didn't know what to expect. When the teacher arrived, I recognized him as someone I'd seen over the years since I'd been in Tucson, and someone who had been a part of the deer dance ceremonies.

Over the weeks, as the class progressed, a friendship was formed between the Yoeme teacher and myself. One night, after the class had ended, we stood in the empty plaza, near the capilla, talking about the beauty of the Sonora Desert and the wonders that abound within it. My friend asked if I ever hiked in the desert and I answered that I did so as often as I could.

At this point, my teacher shared a story with me about the way to enter the desert. A group of people from the Midwest was in Tucson. They were looking for a guide, someone with knowledge of the desert and its flora and fauna. My teacher was asked to take them on a field trip.

On the appointed day, they all met and began to walk, but the mid-westerners, instead of listening to what my friend was saying, cry to the full moon.

The temperature on that summer afternoon was well over one hundred degrees. Before I lit the plants and began my prayers, it had been very still and silent, with only the occasional buzzing of insects. As the flame touched the plants, suddenly the stillness was broken with a chorus of howling. We stood, mesmerized, as we listened to this song seemingly coming to us from every direction. And then, as quickly as it had started, it ended. I know without a doubt that what we heard was not the howling of coyotes. The spirits of the desert were there and when we offered them the incense of the sacred plants, they spoke and responded to our prayers.

Now, whenever I enter the wilderness world, I take time to offer prayers and I walk lightly and with respect upon the earth. Perhaps, had the people who lost their lives in southern Utah, been aware of the importance of entering the mesa country with respect, they would still be alive today.

# CHAPTER 6
# SEEKING

I am humbled that my life has been enriched by the Native people who have reached out and befriended me. My spiritual life has deepened and my perceptions have been immeasurably broadened.

In the early 70s, my wife and I were living in southern Oregon. It was here that I first was introduced to a Seneca elder, a member of the Six Nations Confederacy of the Iroquois (Hau-de-no-sau-nee), also called The People of the Long House. He was far from his traditional homeland in upstate New York. This man became an integral part of my life, changing it forever within a very short span of time.

I can recall vividly the events on the day that we met. While driving through the Rogue River Valley, I was told by a non-native person that this Seneca man did not follow the traditional ways. Over the years, friendships with other Native people have taught me much. I have learned that respect and honor need to be present at the beginning of any friendship. In the traditional way, one shows this respect and honor by taking tobacco as a gift when going to see an elder. Stopping at a small country store, I purchased a carton of cigarettes. If the person was not a traditional, the gift of cigarettes would be viewed as a gesture of courtesy. On the other hand, if this gentleman had been raised in the traditional ways, he would know and understand immediately what I was saying to him.

As I drove into the yard from a long, winding driveway, I was met by a huge tan dog known as Brutus. Sitting on the open tail-gate of a battered pickup truck, sat two men, smoking. Regardless of his beliefs, at least I'd called it correctly on the tobacco. Walking up to the two men, I was introduced and handed the cigarettes to my new acquaintance. The expression on his face was almost one of shock. Sometime later, he told me that no one he knew expressed that type of traditional respect.

Our first meeting lasted for over an hour and a half. The rapport between us was instantaneous. I've often wondered whether it was the tobacco which opened the door. It was as if we had not seen each other in a very long time and we were now renewing an old friendship. A close friend of mine has offered this thought.

He says, "Tobacco is the Creator's gift, a key that allows the two-leggeds to access the sacred world."

Over the months, the friendship grew. Each meeting was a new experience full of insights and teachings. I discovered that my friend stood on neither side of traditional/progressive line. He was simply a lonely old man. His wife had died some years before. He now lived on the property of his sister-in-law and her husband, in a small cabin which they had built for him.

During one of our conversations, he told me that he had a son and daughter who lived somewhere in southern California.

"Somewhere," I asked, "don't you keep in touch with them?"

"My children are ashamed of me because I am an Indian," he said softly, dropping his head. My wife was a white woman."

I was stunned. What could I say? I had no clue as to how to act. The only thing I could think to do was to try and be as good a friends as I knew how to be, giving this friendship whatever commitment was required.

The eye-sight of my friend had been bad for some time. He could no longer drive, so it was up to me to provide the transportation when he came to visit us. My wife and I would invite him to come and stay for the weekend. I would drive out to his cabin on Friday afternoon and take him home again on Sunday evening after supper. These weekends never seemed long enough. While he was with us, he passed on to me information that I know should have been going to a grandchild.

One Saturday, he said to me, "I want to go for a ride."

We drove north toward Roseburg on the Interstate. Turning off onto a state road, we drove up into the mountains, covered with Douglas fir and Ponderosa pine trees.

"We will come to a logging road soon. Take it." My friend now seemed tense and words were terse.

We drove for miles down a rutted road, ferns and dogwood reaching out to us from either side. The track ended near a bald butte. We shut the car off, got out and stood in the bright sunlight. Far below us, the Rogue River wove through the upper reaches of the valley. It glittered silver and gold in the sunlight. A slight breeze swayed through the branches of the trees that surrounded us.

"I want to tell you some things I haven't talked about with anyone for quite a long time," my friend began.

His words remain with me to this day. The story he told me was one I have heard many times since. He told me that he was only part Seneca. His mother's mother was from the Abnaki Nation from the state of Maine. As a young boy, he spent his summers with his grandmother, where she taught him the traditional Abnaki ways.

When he returned to the home of his parents in the fall, he soon learned not to speak about what he had been taught by his grandmother. His mother did not follow the ways of her people. She wanted her son to join the white society. She chided him, angrily, "Don't listen to that old woman. She doesn't know what she's talking about."

My friend paused, a look of pain crossing his face. "I grew up confused. I didn't know what to think. In school, my books said that my people were barbaric savages. Because of my light skin, not many people knew I was an Indian. I was ashamed and I wasn't about to tell them."

I listened to his words silently. It pained me to hear him speak of these things and yet I knew he needed to tell his story.

"I fought in World War II with a lot of other Indians," he said. "We put our lives on the line. And yet, we're still looked down upon." There were tears running down his face. "You and your wife have been most kind to me and I want to thank you in the only way I can."

I put my hand on his shoulder. "Just being our friend is payment enough."

He shook his head and replied, "I've tried to pass myself off as a white man, which was all wrong. We are what we are. The truth is, I've forgotten the old ways that were taught to me by my grandmother. I've forgotten the old words. But one thing is true, I know that the Creator is here with us now, hearing our words and our thoughts."

My friend told me that he knew he didn't have many more years to live. He then told me his ceremonial name and his clan affiliation. With his hand on my shoulder, he said words that are still engraved upon my heart.

"This day, I take you for my son. You are a part of my family and my clan. You have been more of a son to me than the son who is related to me by blood."

I was without words. "Thank you," was all that I could say.

Over the years, I have thought often of the incredible gift this gentle man gave to me. His friendship had no boundaries, no hidden expectations. Is it really so hard for people to open themselves to people of different cultures, different beliefs, different ways of addressing the world and its problems? Is it so hard to be a friend?

A few months later, I found myself in a state of spiritual upheaval. I had to decide whether to move back to upstate New York for serious personal reasons, or to stay in Oregon. I went to my adopted father to ask for his guidance.

"Put together a medicine bag first, and then go on a vision quest," he replied.

My friend and I spent much time together talking about these matters. Once the medicine was collected, I asked how the Seneca or the Abnaki went about seeking a vision. My father replied that I needed to follow the ways of the people on whose land I was now walking.

Given these parameters, there were a number of nations from which I could choose. The people who had lived in the Rogue River Valley, the Tekelma, had been murdered by whites in the late 1800s. The Achomowi, or Pitt River Indians, lived a short way to the southeast, just over the line in California.

These people have a way which they call "In-ill-ah-ah-dew-we." This phrase translates as "gone wandering." When a person is troubled and seeking guidance, he waits until he has been given a sign, and then leaves his family and friends and goes out into the forest to seek answers from the spirits.

I knew no Achomowi. I prayed for guidance and made the decision to go into the forest to seek the answers I needed. Driving into the foothills of Mount Mazama and Crater Lake, I was unsure of what the outcome might be. I had no preconceived idea of where to go. After driving for several hours, I found what appeared to be a small and seldom used state park. Choosing an isolated camp near the river, I got out and gazed at the pines and firs around me. I could see slanting shafts of sunlight, shot through with golden motes of dust. Far in the distance, I could faintly hear the sound of children laughing. I liked the feel of this place. This is where I would stay.

I sat at a picnic table, thinking about why I was here and what I should do next. I had not heard anyone approaching. Suddenly, there beside me was a small boy. He stood, shielding his eyes with his arm, a wilting wild flower clutched in his fist.

"What's your name?" I asked.

"Isidro," he replied.

The young boy offered no further conversation. Squatting in the dust, his black hair shining in the sun, he watched a stink bug as it walked past a scarred pine tree. Soon, I noticed a figure coming toward us through the dappled light and shadows. I recognized him as a Native person with long black hair hanging down his back, almost to his waist. The man called the boy by name. Looking up, Isidro stood, waved his hand, and then went back to bug watching.

When the man reached my picnic table, I stood and introduced myself and offered him a cup of tea from my thermos. We chatted about the beauty of this place, the pleasant weather and other incidentals. I must have shown my good intent. When he was ready to leave, the man set his cup down and invited me to come back down to his camp for dinner. Declining, I explained that I had come here to be alone and to think.

"Come for breakfast then," he said, as he walked away.

Isidro, holding his father's hand, turned, smiled and waved at me.

That night, I lay in my sleeping bag, watching the stars enter the sky. The moon rose late over the tops of the trees, which massed black and pointed against the sky. Far away, I heard the faint sound of music and a spark of light twinkled dimly. I turned and gazed into the slowly dying embers of my fire, thinking about why I was here. Closing my eyes, I slept fitfully, waking occasionally to hear the snap of a branch nearby or the call of some night bird.

Sometime before dawn, I rose and walked to the river, the sound of which had helped to lull me to sleep. Undressing, I bathed in the icy water and felt thoroughly refreshed. I lit a new corn cob pipe from the ember of my fire and offered the smoke to the Four Directions, upward to the Creator and downward to the Earth. As I smoked, I prayed for the guidance I was seeking. When the tobacco had turned to ashes, I returned to my sleeping bag and slept until I was awakened by the sun.

After dressing, I decided to walk along the banks of the river. Rounding a bend, there was Isidro playing next to his father. A warm smile and a hand shake let me know that I was welcome.

"Come and eat with us," Isidro's father said.

I sat on the ground with my back against a huge pine tree. We ate pancakes and freshly caught fish until we could eat no more, and then we sat and talked. As I set my coffee cup down on the ground, Isidro came running over and jumped into my lap.

"Isidro, be polite," Isidro's mother gently scolded him with a big smile.

I kissed the boy's cheek and held him to me, assuring his family that Isidro was being more polite than he knew.

During the long drive down the mountain, I thought about what had happened.

When I returned home, my adopted father asked me, "How was your vision quest?"

He had a big smile on his face, as if he knew what I was going to tell him. After I had explained to him what had happened, he said to me, "You have placed your feet on the Red Road and you have been blessed. Do you feel you have been given an answer to your problem?"

"Yes, thanks to you," I said.

We spent as much time as we could together during the next few weeks. When the parting came, it was filled with both joy and sadness. I was about to journey again to the land of the Hau-de-no-sau-nee and both of us knew that we would probably never see each other again in this life.

Sadly, before the year was over, the sister-in-law of my adopted father informed me that he has passed on to the spirit world. I knew, without a doubt, the quality of the many gifts this man had given to me. With his help and encouragement, I had set my feet more firmly on a path I had been tentatively walking for some years. He has left me with many memories, of a friendship that has blessed me and changed my life forever.

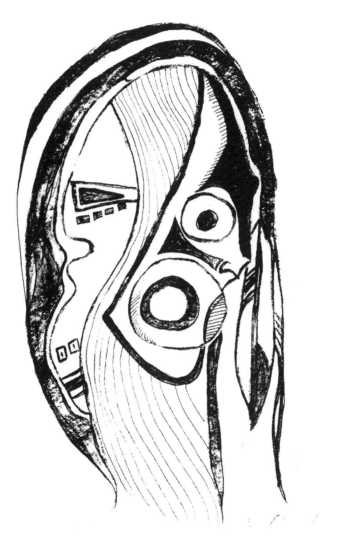

Forest Spirits

Garth NIelsen

The blessings came immediately upon the return of my wife and I to Rochester, New York. There, I had the incredible honor of being welcomed and adopted into the family of a beautiful lady, a Mohawk elder.

In the 1960s, an advertisement in the newspaper caught my eye. It told about a pow wow, the Tonawanda Field Day, held on the Seneca Reservation near Buffalo. Driving onto the reservation, you can see and feel what the country in upstate New York must have been like centuries before the Europeans arrived. The road I was driving got continually narrower and the trees got taller. An occasional log home was tucked beneath the trees.

Suddenly, before me was a large green meadow. I parked and sat down on the grass with my back against a large tree and let the hectic, urban pace slowly slip away. I was offered a cup of coffee and I took this gracious act as an omen of things to come.

The field slowly filled with visitors and vendors of food and craft items. An elderly couple arrived in a loaded van with long tipi poles tied to the top of the van. Immediately, a group of young men approached and untied the poles. They then erected a large, plains-style tipi. Once it was completed, one side was rolled up and a counter was placed in the opening. Iroquois and southwestern silverwork was displayed, along with some of the most beautiful beadwork I have ever seen. A plump and very friendly lady welcomed me to the Tonawanda Field Day.

I wandered around the vendor booths, eating a lot of fry bread, which the Iroquois call 'ghost bread,' and corn soup and watermelon. Somehow, I kept being drawn back to the tipi, standing in its shade to watch the dancers. Here was life being lived in a far different way from what I knew. The friendliness of the people and the beauty of the surroundings were such that I did not want to leave.

For the next six years, each August, I drove to the Field Day. For me, this was a place of emotional and spiritual rejuvenation. I formed a deep and lasting friendship with the elders in the tipi. Each year, we looked forward to our annual reunion. Then, in 1973, my personal life to a major turn and I left New York and returned to Nevada and Northern California.

It wasn't until 1976, after bidding goodbye to my Seneca father that I returned to upstate New York. Once more, I planned a trip to Tonawanda. The weather was warm and clear. Sunflowers lined the country roads. I was excited to be back, especially when I saw the tipi. Here were friends that I had not seen for almost three years. It felt wonderful to be here again.

When my wife and I were about ten yards from the tipi, my friend looked up. Rushing out, she threw her arms about me.

"Where have you been?" she cried. "We thought something had happened to you!"

Walking to the tipi, I explained my absence. Her husband was waiting in the tipi with a big smile on his face. I introduced my wife and we were invited into the tipi.

"Come and sit down. We want to get to know this lady."

By the end of the day, we were all fast friends and my wife and I were invited to come and visit them on the following weekend.

The months turned into years and many visits were made, both to their home on the Tuscarora Reservation and at our home in Rochester. My son was totally entranced by these loving people and thought of them as grandparents.

One day, we received a phone call asking us to come to their home. There was something important to be discussed. When we arrived, we were greeted with hugs and smiles. After a wonderful meal, our friend began to tell a story.

"I was raised in the city of Buffalo," she said. "It was not until I was in my 30s that my mother told me that I was a Mohawk woman. I asked her why she had never told me. She said that the white people would eat me alive if they knew. It's taken my years to play catch-up. You have been a friend and an encouragement to me because you know so much about my people."

She continued, "I spoke to the Council of Chiefs about you. For you see, I want to adopt you as my son."

I felt my knees grow weak with shock. I told her that she honored me greatly. She smiled and said that the Chiefs had told her that there were many honorable white people who had been adopted into the Mohawk Nation. Soon, they said, if this continued, there would be more white people than Mohawks. Because of this, they regretfully declined her request.

One of the Chiefs added, "If this man's heart is good, as you say, he will understand."

I told my friend that just being considered for adoption by her was a great honor.

She said, "Wait, I'm not finished. The Chiefs don't need to know what goes on in the privacy of my own home. Your wife and my husband are the earthly witnesses to these words. This day, I take you as my son. You are now Turtle Clan of the Mohawk."

I was speechless. We all hugged and laughed and cried.

Over the years, our families spent some wonderful times together.

Then, one evening, we received a call filled with sorrow. My Mohawk mother's granddaughter and a friend had been murdered in a drive-by shooting as they walked home. We were asked to come as soon as possible. Upon arrival, my Mohawk mother emerged from the bedroom, her face ashen with grief. My wife and I held her silently for long moments.

"I'm so glad you could come," was all she said.

Going to her room, she returned holding something in her arms. Unfolding it, she showed us a beautiful handcrafted woman's hooded coat.

"I made this for my granddaughter, but she never had a chance to wear it."

Turning to my wife, she said, "I want you to have it."

My Mohawk mother was never the same after the death of her granddaughter. And then, one day, she was gone, returning to her ancestors.

I think often of this kind and compassionate woman. Many years later, at the Big Mountain Sun Dance, I met a Tuscarora man who came each year to dance and pray at this ceremony. When I told him about my Mohawk mother, he jumped up.

"I knew her and her husband," he said. "They once lived near my home."

My blessings from this lady were great and I say this with all of my heart. In the Mohawk language, Jan-Yen-Ga-Ha-Ga means The People From The Hill Where Flint Is Found, or the Flint-Hill People. These were my mother's people. A ho Metakuye Oyasin.

## CHAPTER 7
# SABADO GLORIA

To the majority of people from the dominant society, the Yoeme appear to be acculturated in their forms of religious worship. Although many Yoeme follow the precepts of the Catholic Church, within the religious societies, there are teachings, handed down through the centuries from the time before the arrival of the Spanish missionaries.

According to the Yoeme, Jesus and his mother came to the Rio Yaqui Valley many centuries before the Spaniards arrived in this hemisphere. In this context, the Yoeme were Christian long before they were Catholic. The Yoeme have very distinctive interpretations of the scriptures. The structure of their beliefs and spirituality is unique and totally their own, giving them a different and beautiful world view.

The belief systems of the indigenous peoples of this continent do not contain the concept that issues which are black and white or good and bad, stand in opposition to each other. To Native Americans, the polarities, the dichotomies in life, are essential, needed in order that we may walk between them in balance and harmony.

The Yoeme Easter ceremonies culminate in the celebration of Sabado Gloria, Holy Saturday. This is, for me, one of the most beautiful and spiritually significant ceremonies I have ever witnessed.

Held in the Yoeme barrios and villages, this annual event is attended by large numbers of non-native people. By their actions, it is clear that they are only witnessing what they see as a springtime fiesta. They are largely unaware of the significant spiritual message being played out before them. A play it truly is, in the sense of the medieval morality play.

For all of Lent, the tensions in the Easter drama have been building in intensity. Everything culminates in Sabado Gloria (Holy Saturday).. Before the open capella are piles of leaves and flowers. To the Yoeme, flowers represent blessings. In Arizona, where there are few flowers blooming at Easter time, confetti is used to represent the flowers.

All of the Yoeme religious societies are part of the unfolding pageantry. The members of one of the most unusual societies are called Chapayekas. The individuals in this society wear hand-created helmet masks which parody the world around them. They carry wooden swords and knives which they continually knock together in order to attempt to disrupt the prayers of the faithful. Together with the Soldiers of Rome and the Faraseos, these societies represent the evils which exist in our world. For the Chapayekas, their sense of commitment to these ceremonies is so strong that they hold their crucifixes in their mouths when they wear their masks, so that the evil which they are portraying will not rub off on them, their loved ones or the world around them.

During this Lenten season, these evil ones become continuously stronger and bolder in their mockery of all that is righteous and good. On Holy Saturday, these forces of evil exert their most emphatic effort, trying to overrun the faithful, the capilla and all that is good.

Three times, the evil forces charge the chapel. With each charge, the bells peel wildly from the towers. On the first two attempts, the evil ones are repulsed with a shower of leaves, flowers and confetti.

At the far eastern end of the plaza is a pole. On it is hung the epitome of wickedness, Judas. Just prior to the third charge, all of the evil ones shed their wicked accoutrements in a pile around Judas. They set this pile on fire and flee to the sanctuary of the chapel, amid a shower of leaves, flowers and confetti, representing the blessings of heaven.

From the western perspective, good has conquered evil. Conquest is a European concept. For the Yoeme, this is not the case. My friend, the Yoeme deer musician, told me that rather than conquest, the faith of the people and the goodness they hold in their hearts has converted to good all that has gone wrong, all that is evil. It has brought all things into balance and harmony.

# CHAPTER 8
# SACRED SITES

Over the years, I've had the opportunity to visit sites in the United States that are sacred to many Native peoples. One such site is Wounded Knee in South Dakota.

I had gone with friends to a funeral on the Crow Creek Reservation and we were on our way home to Arizona. In conversation between all of us, it became clear that we felt that it was important to make a stop at this sacred place to pay our respects to the departed.

The accounts of the massacre on that cold winter morning long ago impart the horror and the pain and the suffering of both the Lakota people who died and those who continued to live with that tragic event burned into their memories.

The full impact of that slaughter, now over one hundred years in the past, is, for some Lakota, even today, too painful to recall. But the holders of the sacred traditions: the Wichasha Wakan, the medicine people, the Keeper of the White Buffalo Pipe, the seekers of visions..... they will not let the memory of this event be trivialized by white America into just another chapter in "the Indian wars."

As we walked from the car on that bright autumn day, the full impact of where I was overwhelmed my mind. Standing by the chain link fence which now surrounds the mass grave and the stone monument, I could see innumerable tobacco ties, eagle and hawk feathers, cloth offerings, all hanging from the fence. To me, the offerings became a solid wall of prayer and protection around this holy site. I stood there, my hands resting on the horizontal bar. The feathers fluttered slightly in the breeze and my eyes were full of tears.

"Why, Grandfather," I asked silently.

Walking in the traditional sun-wise Lakota way, I entered one of the gates and stood before the stone monument, reading the names of those who had given their lives for The People. I knelt and touched the stone with my finger, tracing the names. Rising, I placed pinches of tobacco in the four directions. Leaving the enclosure, I went to stand before the grave of Buddy LaMont, the warrior who was killed by FBI agents in the 1973 standoff at Wounded Knee. Again I offered tobacco.

I prayed intently, "Grandfather, let the hatred stop. Let the greed, the prejudice, the misunderstandings and the killings stop. Let your love and peace flow through all of creation once again. Oyate yanipi ktelo. All my relations."

When I returned to the car, my friends were preparing to smoke the chanupa, the sacred pipe. We prayed for peace and understanding, the pipe slowly passing from person to person until only ash remained in the bowl. Our emotions were almost unbearable in their intensity. Not a word was spoken over the miles as we drove home.

I will never forget that day. My feelings, the prayers which were said, the visible impact of an historic event of this magnitude —— are all with me forever. As we drove from the Memorial Site, we paused for a moment at the empty arbor of a Sun Dance circle.

"Let The People live," I said silently in my heart.

Metakuye Oyasin

******

Arizona is blessed with a large number of ancient sacred sites. Many of these sites are still in use by Native peoples of many different nations. Sadly, there are many people who have no respect for the sacred rights of others. The list is discouragingly long of the sites which have suffered the ultimate tragedy of being covered over by asphalt freeways and/or shopping centers.

Shortly after my wife and I moved to Arizona, we made the acquaintance of a long-time resident who told us about one of the surviving sacred sites. This place has been documented as being in use by Native peoples for uncounted generations. It is still being used in a sacred manner to this day.

Over the years, our association with this site has been a blessing, becoming an integral part of our spiritual walk. On each occasion, before entering, we have always offered our prayers and tobacco to the Four Directions. One of our first experiences at this place was of an extremely unusual nature. It had been suggested to us that we might receive a blessing if we were to visit this site at the spring equinox. It was explained that, especially for the people in this desert region, the equinox was a time of great importance, a time for ceremonies, a time for the renewal of life.

We arrived before dawn, while it was still blackest night. I had just shut the engine off and opened the door when, from the northwest, came a huge blue light, streaking across the sky. Flames accompanied the light as it traveled across the sky. We watched in awe as it crashed, soundlessly, into the mountains before us, flames spewing from the impact.

The people in our party all agreed that the impact would be highly visible with the coming of the dawn. Yet, when the sun rose, there was no indication that anything had happened. This event set the tone for what was to follow later that day and, in future visits.

We stood at the center of the ceremonial site waiting for the sun to rise. When it finally crested the mountains, each of us experienced something totally different. Both my wife and I saw figures which resembled the images one sees in a mirage, dancing in the air. These images were clearly visible, yet transparent against the eastern sky.

We all left with little to say. The impact of the experience of that morning has stayed with us throughout the years.

This is clearly a site blessed and guarded by spirits. Within the parameter of the ceremonial center, we have never seen a single rattle-snake. Yet, outside, in the hills surrounding the site, there are a super abundance of desert diamond backs. From a natural standpoint, the presence of so many snakes in one area makes no sense, since rattle snakes are by their very nature, extremely territorial. We have been told by Native American elders that the snakes are there to protect this sacred site.

This site contains many unusual and ancient petroglyphs. Out from the ceremonial center is a huge outcropping of naturally placed boulders which is many stories high. Near the summit of this pile of stones is a small, room-shaped space, formed naturally by boulders which have fallen together. Inside this enclosure are ancient petroglyphs which show the phases of the moon as well as the constellation known as the Pleiades.

Other petroglyphs can be found in the surrounding areas. Among them are a much larger representation of the moon's phases, migration symbols and many different animals and anthropomorphs.

On another occasion, when we were there to observe the summer solstice, we decided to stay the night, just outside the ceremonial area. It was very late at night and we were standing outside our vehicle, talking. Suddenly and soundlessly, from the ceremonial center, we observed a cluster of small blue lights coming horizontally toward us and vanishing just prior to impact. The only explanation we could find was that the spirits of the place were testing us or, perhaps, welcoming us.

I took my friend, the Yoeme deer dance musician, on a visit to this place. He told me that he had heard of this site and was eager to visit and to commune with the ancient spirits of the land. Traveling toward the ceremonial center, our conversations were about the spirits who guard this place. We talked about our individual experiences with guardian spirits. We both felt that this place was welcoming us.

As we walked slowly around the site, I noted numerous badger dens in the area, but did not mention them. We also observed many different offerings which had been left recently.

It was late in the afternoon and we decided to return to my friend's home. As we neared the highway, a badger ran across the road in front of the car. My friend, fluent in the Yaqui language, said that this was possibly a Sewa Huli, or spirit or flower badger. By manifesting himself before us, he was thanking us for visiting his home. I agreed with my friend, reminded of the numerous badger dens we had seen at the sight.

When we arrived at his home, his companion had a delicious meal waiting for us. In the sacred context, the two of us had participated in a ceremony and the eating of a meal is an integral part of the ceremony, completing it and making it whole.

When we finished the meal, we sat in the patio, sharing our thoughts with his companion. Suddenly, coming from the northwest and exploding almost overhead, was an enormous blue light which we all agreed was another confirmation from the spirits. This was their way of welcoming us to that place.

On the following day, we read that a number of other people had observed this phenomenon. University astronomers claimed that this was a meteor and there were monetary offers made for anyone who could find any fragments. To date, nothing has been found.

CHAPTER 9

# WALKING IN BALANCE AND HARMONY

The history books I read in school spoke continually of Native American as being primitive. It is only relatively recently that a small percentage of Euro-Americans have come to the conclusion that there is no such thing as a primitive people. There is now a much broader understanding of the concepts which have shaped the lives of indigenous peoples and the centuries of trial and error which developed their relationship between themselves and the land upon which they lived. It is now understood that to take full advantage of any given local, the people living there must make concessions and adaptations, a process which takes untold perseverance and intelligence.

When speaking of the Native peoples of the Americas, one must understand that the land and the people are one, totally interrelated. We, as interlopers, needs to learn and accept the ancient beliefs and stories of different peoples in this hemisphere who have lived in the same locale for centuries.

Their residence in a particular area has allowed them to develop a "lifeway," which they will tell you comes from the hand of the Creator. This "lifeway" has allowed them to develop a rich and rewarding existence in all levels of life. It enhances their continuity as a people. The adherence to this "lifeway" creates a walk of balance and harmony with all things, and what is done is done for the seventh generation yet to come.

The customs imposed by the dominant society have placed almost insurmountable obstacles in the lives of people who, in the privacy of their personal prayers, have said, "I will not let the ways of my people die with me."

Anglo society needs to take the time to look more closely at the life ways of the indigenous peoples of this continent. The belief that another people is "pagan" or "heathen" needs to be abandoned. It is only when looks at another objectively that truth can emerge.

For instance, the Hopi of northern Arizona have been given exacting rituals, instilled with power from the spirits of the land. Hopi ceremony, like the rituals of other Native groups, is for the people as a whole, rarely for the specific individual. These group ceremonies allow the people to witness the physical manifestations of the event in the form of kachinas. The kachinas have followed the Hopi Votskwani, or Hopi lifeway, without deviation. They have become perfected beings who guide and instruct The People.

In societies that are structured differently than Hopi, cultural and spiritual flexibility has allowed for the emergence of religious practices and songs, chants, ritual ceremonies and remedies for curing through dreams, visions or fasting. Though individually instructed by the spirits in such cases, the instructions given are for the group, not merely for the individual. There are no boundaries between the natural and the supernatural worlds.

The viability of these spiritual practices has enabled many peoples to adapt particular ancient ceremonies to the needs of modern times. For instance, there are a number of Hopi kachinas who no longer make their appearance in ceremonies. Historically, they once played important roles.

The Cherokee now use their war medicine rituals to fight crime. The Cherokee, who have a matrilineal society believe that a vegetable garden is the possession of the woman. Viewed in their terms,

I'Itoi, Baboquvari, Pimeria Alta

Garth Nielsen

this becomes obvious and natural. Women are the bearers of life. They carry the potential for the continuance of life. Who then is better to care for plants which give of themselves for food and medicine, just as a woman gives of herself for the continuity of The People.

Matrilineal groups emphasize the spiritual power of a woman. They stress the idea that a woman's greatest spirituality and power is usually attained after menopause. Within the Hau-de-no-sau-nee, the Iroquois, is the Council of Women, the Clan Mothers, who can both nominate and depose a chief.

It is difficult for Anglo people to comprehend the tie that Native people have with their land. Land, for the dominant society, has become a commodity like cars and washing machines. I once read of a conversation between a Tohono O'odham man and his Anglo friend, that, more than any example I can think of, exemplifies the concept of a "homeland" in Native thought. It is a concept shared by all Native people.

In the conversation, the Anglo man makes references to the ties of the Tohono O'odham Nation to the land. The Native man responds, "See that large mesquite tree over there? I was born beneath it."

That is the knot that binds one to the earth. When this example is multiplied, person by person, generation by generation, the result is a continuous reciprocity between the people and the land, the generations and the land. The land has given of itself in a particular way as a place where The People can center themselves. It contains the birthing places and the graves of the ancestors, who are all around.

When I'itoi, the Elder Brother, of the Tohono O'odham, cleared the land of monsters and cannibals, he gave The People the Law of Life, the Him:dag, and then retired to the holy mountain, Baboquivari. Prior to his departure, he showed the people what plants to use for food and medicine. One of the most important of these plants was the mesquite tree. I'itoi was not only the Elder Brother, but a kinsman endowed with extraordinary abilities, to be sure, but still one of The People.

What person can question the sanctity of the mesquite trees which have always given of themselves with their nourishing beans, that The People might live? Is it not also true that a mesquite tree offered its shade to a mother when her time of delivery had come?

All that is upon the land is made holy in the interconnectedness of life.

If we can recognize that a people and their land are one, and that this is the view taken by this people, than any differences or similarities become irrelevant.

The landscape changes from area to area, but it is landscape which gives form to one's life and spirituality. The response to the environment becomes a response to the Creator. The Creator responds in kind.

I am constantly reminded of the words of the White Buffalo Calf Woman when she brought the Sacred Pipe to the Lakota people: "It is those of good hearts who will be heard by the Great Mystery."

And so it is.

## CHAPTER 10
# MIRACLES

I n the fourth chapter of St. Mark, the Biblical narrative tells that
Jesus wearied of teaching and preaching. Turning to his friends,
gathered near him, he asked to be taken to the far side of the Sea of
Galilee. Part way across the water, a storm suddenly descended on the
boat, with the winds and the waves nearly swamping it.

The narrative goes on to state that Jesus was asleep in the stern of
the boat. Because of the intensity of the storm, his friends became
fearful for their lives. In their consternation, they awoke Jesus and
accused him of not heading the situation or caring for their well-being.
Jesus then stood, and, with a word, calmed the sea to a whisper. Since
childhood, this and other stories place Jesus, in my mind, as someone
with superhuman powers. He was a person who knew secret things
that no one else knew.

As I grew older, that sense of wonder stayed alive within me. I have
always been aware that there are people around us who know things
that others do not know and who can do things which we might call
miraculous. I'm also aware that miracles in the context of the modern
world are viewed with great skepticism. Mainstream thought tells
us that they happened in the Bible, but they don't happen anymore.

As a young boy, I lived in northern Nevada during a period of
severe drought. The high desert of this area was already a very spare

environment, so weather, even hinting of drought, was considered to be a disaster. Things had become grim indeed. Cattle and sheep were suffering and dying, as well as the indigenous wildlife. A few commercial farming enterprises had all but ceased operations due to lack of water. Old timers were resigned and prepared to wait it out.

An article appeared in one of the local newspapers jokingly suggesting that one of the Indian medicine men be asked to do a rain dance. A few days later, a man from one of the eastern Nevada reservations contacted the newspaper, asking if the author of the article was serious about his request.

The person on the other end of the phone at the newspaper stated something to the effect that the country badly needed water quickly and that it mattered little where it came from. Within four days, the rains came, enough to alleviate the drought conditions and provide the needed water. The man whose prayers brought this blessing was barely recognized. A prophet in his own country is never acknowledged.

I can remember feeling a great sense of wonder in hearing of this event. In looking back, I can remember that I had no doubt that this man had been given the power to make it rain. I also could not understand why others did not appreciate or believe that the Creator had caused this miracle to occur through him.

Many years later, in southern Arizona, the infant son of a friend lay in a hospital, fighting for life. For many days, prayers were said for this child's well-being and healing. A few days after his birth, an acquaintance came to our home. He had heard of the child's illness and he suggested that we drive into the desert to a sacred site to pray with the sacred pipe for this little one.

Summers in southern Arizona are as hot as anywhere in the US, and the summers can come early. On this particular day, on a very still afternoon, the temperature was well over one hundred degrees.

The sacred site to which we drove is known to only a few people. Sitting near the center of the site, my friend took out his sacred pipe. Praying in both the O'odham and Indeh (Apache) tongues, he pointed the pipe to each of the four directions, to the sky and to the earth. The stillness around us was complete and the heat was intense. Not a breath of wind stirred.

Suddenly, as he began to fill the pipe with tobacco, into the stillness came a great gust of wind, almost knocking us over with its force.

Strangely, the vegetation around us remained still. The wind vanished as quickly as it had arrived.

Our prayers were said and we left soon after that. But, the thing I can remember is the look on my friend's face when that wind came upon us. He smiled broadly and made a loud exclamation, as if to welcome a friend. I felt then and I feel now that he had called that wind as a confirmation of our intent and a witness to our prayers. There was a sense of wonderment, of being privileged to be present at such an event. I felt that we had been especially blessed because this natural force had been a part of our prayers.

I have spoken elsewhere in these chapters about the Sun Dance. Before going to my first ceremony, I had read as much as I could find on the subject. One of the books said that if a Sun Dance has been planned and it rains, the ceremony is cancelled.

The chill of the misty morning was rapidly replacing the warmth of my sleeping bag as I stood beside my El Camino, drinking coffee from my thermos. The camp was a flurry of activity, with children running around. In the sweat lodge area, last minute instructions were being given to the dancers by the Sun Dance chiefs.

My attention was drawn to the fact that heavy clouds were literally sitting on the land. The tops of the diminutive junipers and pinions were hidden in the mist and everything glowed in a silvery half-light. It felt like the heavens would open up at any minute and the rains would descend. And yet there was no sign that the ceremony would not continue as planned.

I was stepping into a new phase of my life's odyssey, walking into a world that I knew existed, but one that I knew almost nothing of. Reading had barely prepared me for the Lakota Sun Dance I was about to see.

I walked up to the sacred circle and stood with a slowly growing group of supporters around the parameter of the arbor. The top of the Sun Dance Tree was hidden from view by the mist. Only the lower trunk and the cloth offerings were visible.

The singers took their places at the drum and the slow entrance song filled the air. Circling the exterior of the arbor four times, the dancers then entered the eastern gate of the enclosure, led by the two men who were to be the intercessors. The dancers lined up in files while the two chiefs walked to the Tree. Kneeling, they bowed their heads and placed their hands upon the Tree. All the while, the dancers blew upon their eagle bone whistles in rhythm to the drum.

When the two holy men stood, they tilted their heads to the sky and raised their arms toward the east. Their lips were moving in prayer. Suddenly, the low hanging clouds parted and an immense and almost blinding ray of sunlight completely filled the interior of the sacred circle. A loud cry, in unison, rose from the throats of the dancers. The supporters stood transfixed, witnessing this miracle.

In looking back, it seems to me that faith is the key to these events. Faith helps us to believe that the Creator can and does respond to our prayers. But this kind of faith doesn't come easily. We seem to need examples of luminous magnitude to enforce our faith, both at point of contact and in later times of doubt.

We see daily the phenomenon of the natural world around us and we pay little heed to what we have grown accustomed to seeing: storms, wind, rainbows, rain and snow, even the brilliant sunshine. It's when these same events occur out of context that we then place a divine relevance upon them.

The faith of the friends of Jesus was tested by the seemingly lackadaisical attitude toward the storm and their safety. Storms occur frequently on bodies of water. Those who sail upon the water are taught to take heed, to be aware of storm warnings. In this particular instance, the storm caught the disciples unaware and something more was required in their moment of doubt.

The drought in northern Nevada would have ended in time. More people would have been impacted, more animals might have died. In an intersecting point, a miracle occurred, which changed the course of events.

The day at the sacred site was a confirmation that we were standing on holy ground, a place most appropriate for our prayers. The wind became, for each of us, the breath of the Creator, and our faith was reaffirmed.

There are people who view some of the examples I have given as being outside the Christian tradition and therefore as being pagan and/or heathen. I think the time has come to broaden our religious concepts. We need to remove the veil of prejudice from before the eyes of our spiritual intellect.

There's only one Creator of the universe, one God, one Great Mystery.

Each of us sees this entity differently, through the lens of our cultural perspective. The Creator, in like measure responds with our cultural milieu, even though the acts performed may be outside of what we've been taught to perceive as natural laws. When the mist parted with the prayers of the two Sun Dance chiefs, it was to strengthen the faith of all present, I am sure, including themselves.

## CHAPTER 11

# AND THE CHILDREN SHALL LEAD

Afew years ago, I was privileged to attend to performance of young O'odham children dancing the ancient prayers of their ancestors. As is the case with all of the Native nations in arid areas of the far west and southwest, all prayers are ultimately said for rain – "that The People might live." The O'odham follow this tradition, living as they do in a land of few water sources, where blue skies are the norm for nearly 300 days a year.

I sat in the bleachers of the auditorium, watching the children enter and assemble in the center of the room. After their teacher said some private words to them, he spoke to the audience. He introduced the dancers and the dances they would be performing.

The ancient symbols of the O'odham, in black and white earth tones, were painted on the bodies of the small boys. The little girls wore long dresses, once common with their grandmothers. In their hands, the children held cutout representations of rainbows and birds. Dancing in two lines, facing each other, the children danced forward and back. Singing, their small, high pitched voices, carried the message all the O'odham rituals convey: the blessings of rain upon the land. The little voices followed their teacher and their dancing kept cadence with him as he pounded a rattle into his left hand.

They danced three long dances. Three times, the purity of these innocent little ones called down blessings, recalling blessings of another time, singing the songs that have been given to The People.

The fourth dance was one of friendship and thanksgiving. It also was a prayer for rain. The children were now dancing in a large circle, moving counter-clockwise. As they moved in time to the music, the leader stepped to the microphone and once again addressed us.

"Come and dance," he invited us. "This is a time to feel good."

I left my seat and entered the circle, taking a small hand in each of mine.

A couple of days after this event, I was walking through the campus of the University of Arizona. I ran into an acquaintance of mine, a Hopi man who had stopped to chat with several students.

One of the students made a comment that it was very unusual to have rain at this time of the year. It was the end of April and the temperature, during the day, was already over one hundred degrees. The student said that the rain was a relief because it was a refreshing and unexpected blessing.

My Hopi acquaintance said that to the Hopi, this rain, out of season, was a sign that some person, whether an elder or a young child, had prayed with a good heart for the benefit of all – the power of a good heart.

## CHAPTER 12
# DREAMS AND VISIONS

In traditional Native American spirituality, the driving or animating force found in all things is central to all beliefs. The Iroquois call this force Orenda. The Lakota call it Taku Shkan Shkan. For me, it is this force that informs my art.

I was discouraged from accepting any message my dreams held for me as a child. Now, as an adult and as an artists and a writer, and as one who seeks guidance in ceremony, I draw on these dreams and visions as guides for my creative work. Often, these are visions of a long gone reality which now requires recognition in this time. As such, my efforts have become a place of centering in my life, and it is a tremendous release for me to be able to translate these visions graphically.

I feel that I can honestly say that it is only since my involvement with the ceremonies I have privileged to witness and be a part of that I have gained the ability to reach deep into the natural world. I feel I can now unite what I see with mind and spirit.

As an artist, I need to try and illustrate the innate spirituality in my life and to create an image of the spirit within me. In this creative process, I am graphically portraying what is sensed and intuited.

For me, in both my paintings and my writings, logic is not all that important. I want to be continually reminded of the magic in life that logic can often hide. I recognize this magic as that same animating force found universally in Native American beliefs. It gives life and art meaning. It clarifies my own private and very personal myths and gives structure to my beliefs.

I find magic in nature as well. I can experience awe at the sight of a magnificent rainbow after a downpour. I can feel the presence of the Creator in witnessing a flash flood in the desert. I can see the unblemished beauty of a majestic mountain glistening after a blizzard. To view the rapid transformation of a seed into a plant, the effortless gliding of a hawk or a fossil embedded in a stone is to not only realize one's own mortality, but one's interconnectedness with all life. These are the things that connect us with our dreams and visions and make us what we are.

The act of creating, for me, is not something outside of myself. It has become that thing by which I define myself. As a farmer is his fields and his crops, he is both the effort and the end result. My art has become my life. More importantly, it becomes the means by which I am able to communicate with the Creator and He with me.

## CHAPTER 13

# HOMES

As a child, I was always intrigued by the homes of Indian people in my picture books. I was overjoyed when I found out the museums held reproductions of them. It was very early in my life when I was introduced to the wonders hidden behind the walls of museums of natural history. I can recall the wonder that I felt viewing the dioramas in the Southwest Museum in Los Angeles. Then, when my parents moved to Reno, Nevada, every visit to the Nevada State Museum in Carson City was a renewed adventure.

The cultural artifacts of the Native peoples of the Americas held my interest like nothing else. As I stood gazing through the glass at some display, it was as if I could transport myself as well as what I was looking at back to the place of origin. The adults around me always accused me of having too vivid an imagination. I could never figure out why this wasn't a good thing. Using it, I felt that I was able to understand what I was looking at much more clearly.

For the almost twenty years that I lived in Rochester, New York, one of my favorite and most pleasurable pastimes was to visit the Rochester Museum and Science Center. The second floor was the level devoted to both archaeology and anthropology. There was a reconstructed Seneca log home from the eighteenth century.

Peering through the screened window in the door, the viewer is made privy to the rapidly changing world of the Iroquois people during the 1700s. The man and the woman wear clothes made of European cloth. Some metal pots hang on hooks or sit near the fire. The woman pounds corn in the traditional, upright tree stump mortar. Other indigenous artifacts in this diorama complete the interior of this small home. It was easy for me to imagine the entire setting, not inside some white man's modern building, but in a setting like Tonawanda or Allegheny, with maple and basswood tress turning red or yellow in the fall.

When I moved to Arizona, I became acquainted with a most exceptional man. He knew all there was about how to survive on your own. He taught me how to knap flints. He could make fire with hearth sticks. One afternoon, I watched him gather coyote fur from bushes as we walked in the desert. He said that later, he would turn this fur into yarn to be used in a blanket or clothing. At the time, he was the world champion atl atl thrower. He had been hired some years before to take talented students and teach them desert survival skills. What he did was to have his students build a reproduction of an O'odham pit house. Pit house remains have been found throughout the southwest. These are what the people lived in prior to the advent of the Pueblo culture. They are semi-subterranean buildings, oval in shape, usually no more than three feet below the surface of the ground. Two large forked logs provide the end posts, over which are placed mats and brush. Many times, a covering of caliche is applied to make the structure waterproof.

When my friend took me to see the reconstructed pit house that he and his students had built, he told me that not one metal object had been used in the creation of this home. Everything had been done as the ancient people must have done it.

To enter this home is take a quantum step backward in time. For me, when I first walked into this small house, all the hairs on the back of my arms stood up. There is an aura of ancientness about the place. Even though indigenous people never lived in this house, they lived on this land and their spirits seem to be present in this place. It is truly an amazing site.

Quite a number of years ago, my wife and I were attending the Big Mountain Sun Dance. On the night of the first day, as we lay in our tent, suddenly, across the night air came the sound of rattles, singing and the beat of a water drum. For a brief moment, I couldn't discern what was happening. I knew that the intercessor for the Sun Dance was also a road man for the Native American Church. We unzipped our tent flap and peaked out. The tipi where the ceremony was being held was about twenty yards away. The upper half of the tipi was pale white against the night sky. The lower half was illuminated from within by the center fire. Shadowy figures of the celebrants were silhouetted against the canvas.

The ceremony lasted all night. The soft singing, accompanied by the rattles and the drum, put us to sleep. I recall saying to my wife that I felt like I had stepped back in time. It didn't take much to imagine what it must have felt like to live in a gathering of The People on the Great Plains. To this day, the tipi represents a place of worship.

My good friend, Peter, arrived in Tucson to see his father. He also wanted to do some exploring. A couple of days after his arrival, he called and asked if I could get away for a few days. He wanted me to take him on a trip north to the Hopi and the Dine reservations.

"Are there things to see on the way?" he asked.

It was early afternoon when we drove into the parking lot at Casa Grande National Monument, the ancient ruins of the Hohokam People. This was the beginning of a five day trip back in time, a trip into the world of the First Ones.

We walked slowly about the old adobe and caliche walls and we spoke of the meanings of this place and the ones who had built it. Where had they gone? The archaeological records indicate that they left around 1400. As I placed my hands on the walls, the tiny stones in the caliche all but called out to me in an audible voice of some unknown mystery. Even with the tourists and their chatter in the distance, the silence of the desert bore down upon this place. The smell of shu:gya (creosote), the ancient medicine plant of the Tohono O'odham, was pungent on the air.

We walked to where the old ball court lies, still unexcavated. As we stopped and looked around us, my eyes were drawn to the ground. There, a tiny shard lay, as if in a grand mosaic. Here was a small piece of someone's heart and soul. Was this once a bowl used by a medicine person? Was pinole once cooked in this vessel?

As we drove down into the Verde Valley, a huge expanse opened before us, with jagged mountains guarding the north and cottonwood trees lining the Verde River. At the northern end of the valley, we took the turn off to an ancient marvel of architectural engineering. We walked from the car into the alcove cut through the centuries by Beaver Creek. A large grove of sycamore trees was sheltered by canyon walls that rose precipitously above our heads.

As we rounded a bend in the black-topped path, there, high above us, hung the complex known as Montezuma's Castle. Tucked into the cliff's overhanging brow, the magnitude of these dwellings is wondrous.

Early European settlers in this area had no knowledge of the original peoples in this area. When they came across these magnificent ruins, they immediately jumped to the conclusion that they must have been built by the Aztecs. Hence, we now have these inappropriate names for sites in this area.

Boulders littered the talus beneath the dwellings, interspersed with undergrowth. A quiet pervaded this place which seems different from the surrounding desert. Here was a place of prayer, centeredness and belonging. We felt we were being held by invisible hands and we didn't want to leave this ancient spot of beauty and spirit.

Archaeological evidence indicates that the Sinagua had extensive gardens down along the edges of Beaver Creek. We stood next to the creek, looking back up at these cliff dwellings. What must it have been like to live here on this incredibly beautiful land? Who did these people fear and why did they feel that needed to build their homes in these high, inaccessible, wind-carved caves?

Eleven miles further up Highway 17 is another sacred place, a cenote, a place of ceremony, Montezuma's Well. As we walked the curving, narrow path going down to the well, we stopped and looked up and across to the far side. Adobe and caliche homes still cling within the sheltering niches. Their windows seemed to be like dark eyes staring out at us. Further down the path, adobe bricks outlined the foundations of more ruins.

Below us, all was in stillness, but for a small flock of ducks which swam in the cenote, calling to each other. The coming dusk cast long shadows on the walls of the well. It was easy to conjure in my mind's eye the activity which once must have taken place in this spot.

It is obvious that this was never a heavily populated area. The dwellings are few in number. What was this place? Were the people who lived here the guardians of this spot? Was this a place of sacredness and ceremony, containing, as it does, the water of life in this desert area?

Going east, we left Flagstaff. We would soon enter villages with names from another time, full of meaning: Polacca, Kykotsmovi, Oraibi, Walpi, Shongapovi, Moenkopi, Shipalovi. Registering at the Visitor's Center, we waited for a guide to take us on the tour of First Mesa. Inside this tiny room, there were a number of elderly Hopi ladies weaving baskets. We stepped outside to feel the cool morning air.

An aged woman walked slowly up to us and welcomed us to her village. She asked if we would like to come to her home to see the pottery she had made. We were both struck by the honor which we felt was being extended to us by this Hopi lady. The small room we entered was like nothing we had ever seen. The sandstone blocks were chinked with mud plaster. The roof beams, brought from the San Francisco Mountains, and the flagstone floor, both spoke of great age. We were standing within a home in a village which is among the oldest continually inhabited villages in North America.

We talked with this gracious Hopi woman, commenting on what it must be like to wake up each morning and look out across the 600 foot drop off at the edge of the mesa and out into the infinity of the great expanse of the northern desert. To us, the idea of living in this place was overwhelming. Clearly, to live here was to participate in an entirely different way of being.

In 1680, when the pueblos of the Rio Grande Valley revolted against Spanish rule, many of the Spanish oppressors were either killed or fled back to Mexico City. Some of the pueblo peoples thought that they had won this war. Others were not so sure. A group of Tewa speaking people made the decision to travel north to their Hopi allies to ask for sanctuary.

Today, on First Mesa, in extremely close proximity on this small finger of stone, three villages exist: Hano, Sitsomovi and Waalpi. The people, who speak two totally different languages, work side by side in harmony, supporting each other in the calendrical round of sacred ceremonies. To the outsider, they appear as one.

## CHAPTER 14
# THE WAY OF
# THE WARRIOR

The Iroquois call themselves Ongkweongwe, which means "The Real People." On first glance, this may not be understood by outsiders. A deeper meaning must be discovered.

To be a real person in traditional Iroquois culture is to do and be a part of many things. People must first know their customs and their histories. They must follow the Gaiwiio, known to the whites as the Code of Handsome Lake.

They must live by the Great Law of the Creator. This law, in its simplest form, states that Native people are the care-takers of the earth, Turtle Island. This care-taking includes care of not only the green and growing nations, but the lakes, rivers and streams, the four-leggeds, the wingeds and those which creep and crawl – all living among us.

This obligation of caring for the earth is a central tenant for every indigenous nation in the hemisphere. Native beliefs enable the people to inhabit the eco-system in which they live in a way that does not allow for over exploitation and exhaustion of the resources which surround them. In talking with Native elders I have known over the years, it is my understanding that one cannot be a real person without a genuine love of the earth and all that is upon it.

Recently, there have been a number of books and articles criticizing those who speak for the Native American reverence for the earth.

These attacks cite events like the Buffalo Jump kill off in the Midwest, where piles of bones indicate a massive slaughter of animals by Native Americas prior to the arrival of the whites. These attacks state that no small group of people could have possibly used that much meat or to have been capable of transporting this meat to other locations prior to the advent of the horse.

I find this type of reasoning disturbing for two reasons: it indicates a lack of understanding of Native American ways on the part of the authors and it implies that the authors did not do much research in this area.

Historical documentation and present practices indicate that when traditional people kill an animal, every single part of the animal is used. Nothing is wasted. A Dakota friend told me that when a buffalo is slaughtered and processed, there is not even enough for the ants to carry away. Never is an animal killed for trophy. Never is an animal killed for just the heart or the tongue or the hide. Native tradition and spirituality state that all animals are their relations. They do not view the killing of an animal as another type of harvesting of crops. Life is sacred and taken only after prayers have been said.

Historically, a massive, organized group effort could easily have handled the processing of huge amounts of meat and other animal products. Extensive trade networks extended throughout the continent. Such trade networks could easily have been used to distribute large amounts of food as a trade item. Again, nothing would have been wasted. This respect for all of our relations is still with us.

Some years ago, my wife and I met a young Yoeme man. We saw each other frequently over the months and he began coming over to our home to share a meal and long evenings filled with conversation.

One evening, he told us a little about his background. He said his family lived in northern California and that his father was a successful business man. He had been raised with no knowledge of his traditional Yoeme heritage and had come to Arizona to try and learn about his people.

Southwest of Tucson is a Yaqui Reservation called Pascua Pueblo. It was here that our young friend went to explore his roots. He was welcomed by the elders of the village and he began studying with a spiritual advisor. During this period, he was initiated into one of the religious societies. He spent much time with the children, working with them in programs designed to help them learn their traditional ways and to fight against the social problems confronting third world children: drug addiction, suicide, alcohol addiction, gang membership, poverty and lack of education.

As elders, our friend often came to us to discuss problems and what the future might hold for his people. We spent many evenings taking about the revolution in Chiapas and how it had impacted on the indigenous peoples of the hemisphere. We also shared some very private and meaningful ceremonies with this remarkable young man.

And then, one morning, we received a phone call from a mutual acquaintance telling us that our friend had been arrested and taken into custody by the FBI. We were in a total state of shock. It took some time to sort out the details.

In talking with his parents, we began to understand a little more about our friend. His mother told us that even when he was a very young boy, he sought to understand the differences among people. Raised in a family with a strong spiritual background, he told us, they told us that as he grew into his teens, he knew there was something missing in his life, but he didn't know what it was or how to find it.

He had always had a great love for animals and a great aversion for any who caused suffering for these relations. His heart was grieved by what he saw happening to the animals of this world, especially in areas of scientific research and experimentation, because these little ones were helpless and had no advocate.

He had joined some high profile animal rights organizations. He put together a film on practices used by the fur industry in harvesting pelts. It was later shown on a prime time television news program and was largely responsible for exposing the intolerable cruelties used in this industry. The film, shown widely, was also responsible for a significant dent in fur industry sales.

In the FBI indictment, the federal government stated that our friend was wanted for what they termed "terrorist acts." I have a hard time figuring out how government attorneys defined this term. In all of his activities, this young man never once killed or harmed a single human being or animal. The only thing he did was to advocate for the human treatment of the animals of the world. In so doing, he interfered with US commerce and the flow of cash into multi-national coffers. This was his crime.

Pre-trial hearings were held in Tucson, Arizona. Our friend was kept in high security and appeared in court in manacles and handcuffs. He was denied bail because the federal government considered him to be a flight risk. From the number of federal agents around him at all times, one would have thought he was a serial murderer or a rapist.

The trial was held back east. It soon became apparent that the federal government had very little actual evidence against our friend. As a result, the government offered him complete amnesty if he would divulge names of his friends, dates of activist events and detailed descriptions of all activities in which he'd been involved for the last ten years.

"This is not the Indian way," our friend said to the federal judge. "Indian people are loyal to their friends. We do not rat on each other." This brave Yoeme man chose to serve time in a federal prison, behind "the iron door," rather than be disloyal to his spiritual beliefs.

Just before he was taken away, he said to me, "Uncle, pray for me. Thank you for standing beside me. All my relations."

Though not an Iroquois, but a traditional Yoeme, this young man stands tall against the environmental slaughter of the earth and those who walk on four legs.

He epitomizes the phrase, Ongkweongwe!

## Chapter 15

# Shadows On the Spiritual Path

I've had some wonderful friendships over the years. These are people who have had a major impact upon my thinking and the course of my spiritual walk on the earth. Some of these relationships have lasted only as long as a cup of coffee and a cigarette. Some have matured and grown over the years. All have been a blessing to me.

The lessons I have received from these friends have been many and they have enabled me to look at myself and my society with new eyes. In incorporating these teachings into my life, I've spent much time looking at my own culture, my own beliefs, my own morality. I find in western civilization something that has been weighed in the balance and found wanting.

In chaotic times, God calls forth individuals with the strength, courage and abilities to stand vigilantly against the tide of inhuman brutality. Such a man was Bishop Samuel Ruiz Garcia, the now retired prelate of San Cristobal de las Casas in the state of Chiapas, Mexico. I had the great honor of meeting and talking with this gentle man in 1994 when I was a member of the Pomo Peace Caravan.

His life was in constant danger from those who sought to disrupt the peace process between the EZLN and the Mexican government. While we were in San Cristobal, we learned that Bishop Ruiz could go nowhere without a body guard because of constant threats to his life.

The UPI reported many assassination attempts against the churchman. In one account, he was returning from a pastoral visit to a small, isolated village in Chiapas when armed gunmen attacked his caravan. No one was killed, but several of his people were wounded. The account concluded by speculating that the gunmen had probably been hired by PRI, the most powerful political party in Mexico, prior to the Vicente Fox. Attacks had also been made against bishop Ruiz's sister. In one incident, she was beaten almost to death.

Bishop Ruiz strove to be a man of the people and to walk in Christ's footsteps. He spoke at least seven different languages including Tzeltal and Totzil, two of the indigenous Mayan languages of Chiapas.

While the Pomo Peace Caravan was in San Cristobal, all of us had a private audience with Bishop Ruiz. As I shook hands with him, he said words which still resonate in my memory.

In heavily accented English, he said "There is no person on the face of the earth who can keep me from my promise to Christ. I will feed the hungry. I will clothe the naked and care for the sick. I will sucker the widows and the orphans. They will have to kill me to stop me."

The Maya people of Chiapas adore this man, who made no distinctions between himself and his people. They call him a saint and with good reason. Daily, he put his life on the line.

Some years ago, I spoke with an indigenous elder about Bishop Samuel. He said, "Biology is not the only determining factor in a person's makeup. It is how one thinks and acts, how one views the world and the life we've been given, that matters. What I'm saying is this: to be an Indian is not simply to just have red skin and black hair. To be a true person, by traditional definition, is to daily show compassion and love for all of creation."

Bishop Ruiz meets these standards. Over and over again, he acted as a mediator between the EZLN and the Mexican government, traveling all over Chiapas to attempt to effect resolutions. As a man of the cloth, he did much to prevent needless bloodshed. He became an advocate for the Maya People, who fought for their basic human rights. As such, he was nominated for the Nobel Peace Prize on numerous occasions. He was a man who refused to allow anything to stand in the way of his spiritual commitment. In my mind, he represents what western civilization could or should be.

*******

I have a Lakota friend who is a Sun Dancer, a spiritual leader who serves his people well. Like Bishop Ruiz, he stands tall and strong for The People. He is a living picture of spiritual commitment. When he talks, his words come not just from his heart but from the depths of Lakota wisdom and from the Great Mystery.

He and his family have honored my wife and I by coming and sharing a meal and an evening with us. In traditional ways, sharing a meal is a sacred ceremony unto itself. I have also been honored at a private sweat lodge ceremony which he conducted. This sacred ceremony was unique and spiritually powerful because of the ancient objects which were an integral part of this renewal.

One night, my friend and I sat and talked about the Pomo Peace Caravan. While we had been in Chiapas, we were asked by a representative to speak for the Maya People and for the desperate conditions under which they live on a daily basis. We were asked to relay their request for help and support to their indigenous brothers and sisters across the border in the north. I was given a video tape and a specific message to relay to the Lakota People. My friend listened with respect and told me that his people would respond.

Our conversation turned to Anglo involvement with Native people today. Traditional prophecies have spoken for years of a time when the white man would come to help his indigenous brothers and sisters. My friend spoke of the blessing that some white people have brought to the Lakota.

"Long ago," he said, "when my people were being killed by the US cavalry, there were some white people back east who were against the slaughter of Native Americans. They lobbied in Washington DC to end these genocidal practices. Enough pressure was applied and the outcry was loud enough to reverse governmental polies to some extent. Today, Lakota people still walk on the earth because of these compassionate white people. We owe these people our lives. Perhaps, this is what the Pomo Peace Caravan has done for the Maya People."

Here is another man who walks the path of spiritual commitment. He has taught me well.

In this time of drive-by shootings and casual terrorism, to walk a committed, spiritual path is to walk in constant danger, to walk on the edge. Here are people who put their lives on the line on a daily basis. To be a spiritual spokesperson for Third World Nations in a First World environment is to make oneself vulnerable, a highly visible target to all who seek to control minority peoples.

## CHAPTER 16
# WALKING ON THE EDGE

Afriend and I were returning to Tucson from Phoenix, using the old Casa Grande Road. We had been driving in silence for some time when my friend said to me, "Turn around and go back to that wide spot in the road."

I turned the car around and drove back. To me, there was nothing to see except mesquite and cholla. Getting out of the car, my friend walked to the barbed wire fence that lined the road and unhooked a whole section of the fence. He waved his hand at me, indicating that I should drive the car through the opening. He reattached the fence and got back into the car.

"Follow the dirt tracks," he said.

We drove a short distance, when, suddenly, there ahead of us, was a most unusual site. We were at what the O'odham call "The Children's Shrine."

My friend said, "Because you've helped my people and you've always been very respectful of traditional Native ways, I wanted to bring you to this place."

We stood in silence and then my friend began to pray in the O'odham language. I took out tobacco and offered a pinch to the four directions, the heavens, the earth, and pinch on the shrine itself. When his prayer was completed, we stood in silence and then returned to the car without speaking.

As is the case with many sacred sites, there are several versions extant as to why the O'odham venerate this place. According to one version, a water serpent monster once lived in the springs and streams in the homeland of the O'odham. Somehow, this monster was offended by the people. It then caused the waters to overflow their normal courses so that it began to flood the land. People began to flee to higher elevations and still the waters rose.

The monster declared that it would only be appeased by the sacrifice of two children. The water continued to rise and the people were fearful. They could not even begin to understand how they would be able to make such a sacrifice.

Finally, when it appeared that all was lost, according to this version of the story, a young girl and boy were sacrificed to the monster. Immediately, the waters receded.

In another version, tradition says that the stones of "The Children's Shrine" cover a hole in the earth. Once, long ago, through this hole, ocean waters threatened to flood the land of the O'odham. In this version, the flood was stopped by the sacrifice of four children, a boy and a girl from each moiety. They were thrown into the hole, but remain alive underground to this day.

Even with examples like Christ, who was totally selfless, standing before them, western societies stress the absolute importance of individuality. Native societies, on the other hand, see things from the opposite end of the spectrum. Over and over again, in traditional indigenous teachings, stories like these of "The Children's Shrine" are told to show the necessity of person sacrifice for the benefit of all the people.

The man who stood beside me that day at "The Children's Shrine" exemplifies this type of sacrifice. He travels thousands of miles a year in rez vehicles (the kind that are ready to fall apart at any moment) on unpaved roads on both sides of the border. He travels to isolated villages that aren't even shown on the maps. Using his own meager income, he spends weeks away from his family and friends. What he's doing for his people is not easy. Traveling through heat and cold, he often sleeps in his car because of lack of funds and the fact that there's no place available for him to find lodging.

A multi-lingual man, speaking three languages, he talks for his

I'ltoi, The Man in the Maze

Garth Nielsen

people, who live on the verge of extinction. He speaks for the sacred sites of his people, located on both sides of the international border, which are daily being vandalized and lost. He speaks for the land and the water, the plants and the animals, all of which are integral for the survival of The People. Multi-national mining interests are polluting the land and the water. Because of the harsh desert environment, these inappropriate techniques are destroying fragile, priceless ecological systems which can never be replaced.

Caught between two countries, divided among themselves, his people have very little voice in their own future. In Mexico, they have no local school, no medical facilities, no social services of any kind. Compounding the daily fight for existence, across their lands, uninvited, come the drug runners.

The drug runners are not the only ones traveling across O'odham land. Because of the 1994 indigenous revolution in Chiapas, there are now refugees fleeing oppression and persecution, seeking asylum in the United States. A large percentage of them come across O'odham lands. Because of this, a militarized zone has been created all along the US border. Both the Mexican and the US governments have continually abused the rights of the O'odham by invading their homes without search warrants. They routinely stop and search O'odham vehicles and use threats and intimidation. In many cases, there is real question was to whether the "officials" involved have actually been authorized by any governmental agency.

With no sources of income and a disrupted life style, the O'odham on the Mexican side of the international border are caught between wanting to stay on their traditional homeland and trying to survive. They are being forced to leave their traditional lands to seek employment within First World societies. When they leave their land unprotected, in their absence, it is being stolen by outsiders or burned to the ground. When this happens, the people have little or no redress.

Caught in the middle, the O'odham are now denied access to their own families, their own land, their own ceremonies, to their very existence as a people. Unless they jump through hoops that involve three languages, and multiple layers of governmental red tape, they no longer have the right to free access across the border. They are losing their Him:dag, their life way, their sacred sites, their land, their culture, their language and the very essence of their identity as O'odham.

My friend has dedicated his life to his people, speaking out to anyone who will listen on these issues. He lives daily with the threat of death. There has been over five hundred years of the denial of basic human rights, misunderstandings, hatred and the shedding of blood upon this land. The stories of "The Children's Shrine" speak of the giving of one's life for the good of The People. Will my friend's life be required as the ultimate sacrifice in order to stop the flood of oppression which now threatens to overwhelm the O'odham?

## Chapter 17

# Inipi

Inipi – the dwelling where breath is made.

The sweat lodge, or inipi, in the Lakota language, is a sacramental rite associated with prayers. The sweat, though usually a communal experience, is, none the less, an intensely personal one.

I had read for years of the use of the sweat lodges by Native people. The sweat, in one form or another, is utilized by nearly all Native peoples of the hemisphere. It is the traditions of the Lakota and other Great Plains people with which I am most familiar.

My first experience was in 1984 when my wife and I had moved from upstate New York to Arizona. I had made the acquaintance of a man who was a Sun Dancer from the Winnebago, or Hochunk Nation. We were both working for a residential center for abused children. Our conversations began to focus on Native people. When an invitation to attend a sweat was offered, I accepted and reread all the information I could find on this ceremony.

The ceremony I was invited to was held at night and I was told to arrive early so that I could be instructed on what was going to take place and what I was to do.

I was shown how to make chanli wapti, tobacco prayer ties. These, I was told, were to be placed in the willow framework over my head when I had settled myself within the sweat lodge. The man who was to pour the water was a Cree from Canada, an elder who was shown much respect by those in attendance.

When the stones were well-cooked and the men began to undress, I saw that they all had long hair, down nearly to their waists. What startled me most were the scars on the chests of all of the men. When I had walked to the lodge from the house that night, the only light was from the fire heating the twenty-eight stones. I was the only Anglo in the ceremony. The other men were all members of various Native Nations. There were about a dozen or so of us. Realizing that I was in the company of Sun Dancers, I was on edge and unsure of whether I should even be there. But it is my nature to try and finish whatever I begin, so I stayed. I later learned that to leave a tradition Native ceremony is to dishonor that ceremony.

When the flap door was closed after the red hot stones had been brought in, all was quiet and the glow from the stones cast a reflected image on us all. Fragrant herbs were sprinkled on the stones as well as tobacco, filling the lodge with an aroma that was pleasant and settling. The herbs twinkled like stars in the darkness.

Slowly at first, then more vigorously, the water was splashed on the stones and the heated steam swirled up and around us. Ancient chants were sung and seemed to touch something deep within me. That "something" can only have been my spirit, which responded in a way that can only be described as reaching out to the chants. I was being drawn in totally to this ancient way of prayer.

I would be less than honest if I didn't say that I was fearful and a little intimidated by both the men I was with and by the ceremony itself. But, upon reflection afterwards, I came to realize that this was another step on the Red Road upon which I was being led, and that my adoption by my Seneca father had brought me to this point in my life. It was the Spirit which first manifested itself to me so long ago in the deserts of northern Nevada which pointed me in this direction.

Drumming and Chanting Filled The Darkness

Garth Nielsen

## CHAPTER 18
# PRAYING DOWN THE RAIN

As I've mentioned several times in these chapters, it is well known that Arizona summers can be excessively hot. The drought in the 1980s exacerbated this situation with dire results. Livestock and indigenous animals suffered severely on the Joint Use Land Area of the Dine/Hopi Reservations.

The annual Sun Dance was then being held at Big Mountain. The courage and spiritual inspiration of not only the dancers, but the support people, was manifestly apparent. To participate in this ancient and beautifully fulfilling ceremony was courageous, to say the least.

The intercessor, a Lakota man of a quiet yet strong spiritual strength, led the ceremony without any indication of wavering in his commitment to his belief in Wakan Tanka or to the men and women for whom he was responsible.

Many Dine elders stood among the support people under the arbor surrounding the sacred circle on the third, and for most, the hardest day of the ceremony. A spokesperson representing those Dine who were resisting the partitioning of the land had come to the intercessor prior to the ceremony that day, requesting prayers for rain to bless this parched land. The intercessor was told that both plants and livestock were perishing. He listened and a promise was given.

During the hottest part of the afternoon, the intercessor, with assistance from his sub-chiefs, brought buckets of water into the circle. Those familiar with the Lakota Sun Dance are cognizant of the fact that the dancers neither eat nor drink for four days. For water to be brought into the circle seemed, to some, to be a travesty, a conflict. The intercessor had an entire eagle wing fan which he used in all sacred ceremonies. This fan, he now dipped into the water buckets held by his assistants. He flung the water first upon the sacred tree, then upon the thirsty dancers, who stood transfixed, with open mouths, catching the drops as they were flung about. The people beneath the arbor were also blessed with "the water of life." This continued for almost an hour and then my wife touched my arm and pointed to the southwest.

For many weeks, the skies in Arizona had been a bright turquoise blue. But now, a small white cloud was slowly moving in our direction. As we watched both what was taking place within the sacred circle and the sky, the cloud grew in size. Within an hour, the entire sky was filled with grey clouds. With a clap of thunder, it began to pour down rain.

The Dine elders who stood near us had tears streaming from their eyes and their hands were held upward as they prayed, giving thanks. And so the drought was broken and the people and the land, with all the life upon it, were refreshed and all was brought back into harmony.

## Chapter 19

# Who Is My Neighbor
# Who Are My Realtions

The road wound in lazy curves, rising and falling in undulating, roller coaster rises and dips. Bare, jagged rock outcroppings and fierce mountains jutted upward from the desert floor, near at hand and rimming the horizon. Baboquivari Peak, the home of I'itoi, the Monster Slayer, rose above the other peaks like a gigantic thumb. I was passing through the very center of the Pimaria Alta, the heart of the Tohono O'odham homeland.

We were on the road in response to a commitment I had made about a week earlier. I had attended a benefit dinner for a newly formed organization of Native people from northern Sonora and southern Arizona. During the evening, I talked with my host and told him that I would be honored to be of service to him and his people in any way he felt was beneficial.

Several days later, I received a phone call. My friend spoke, asking for my help, telling me of an urgent need. An elder, an O'odham-Yoeme woman, had been brought to Tucson from one of the border villages in Sonora for medical treatment. Her illness had been diagnosed as terminal cancer. Her leg was swollen and ugly. The doctors could do nothing to help her. She was being sent home to die.

The woman was terrified by all of the gringos who did not speak her language in these strange surroundings. The pain in her body showed clearly on her face. Her skin was pulled tightly across her skull. Her eyes looked at me dully, and she cried out in her pain as we placed her in the back of my SUV as gently as we could. The two Anglo nurses, who had wheeled her from the hospital to the car, wore forced smiles of strained professionalism. This Indian woman had touched something inside of each of them, but they couldn't let it show.

Driving into the BIA town of Sells, Arizona, we stopped at the Agency Headquarters and then drove to a filling station for gas. The day was hot and a strong wind blew the burning air into our faces as we stood beside the car, drinking sodas. Inside the car, the old woman's daughter sipped a drink and watched over her mother.

Driving into the border crossing, my friend, speaking Spanish, told the officer why we were there. We were waved through without comment.

Except for the black top roads and the ever-present billboards, the village consisted of old and crumbling adobe buildings. I could have been in the nineteenth century.

The woman's daughter, who had been silent during the entire trip from Tucson, now told us where to turn from the main road. We followed a dirt track that twisted and turned randomly around houses in various stages of decay and collapse. To me, utter hopelessness seemed to bare down on the whole place. I was reminded of the book, The Plumed Serpent, by D. H. Lawrence.

The rutted road ended at a ramada with ocotillo canes for walls. The roof was covered with blanket fragments, old tarps and dried palm fronds, which shaded the interior. The packed earth floor was cool. Cats, dogs and chickens wandered through the spaces between the ocotillo canes. A small ditch ran in front of the door. Boards had been placed over the ditch, which was filled with brown, oily looking water.

A man, disheveled and dirty, came to the car, crying at the sight of the old woman. Stooping to kiss her forehead, he said in Spanish, "Momma, you are home." Tears streamed down his cheeks.

My friend and I carried the elder from the car to a wheelchair, which the woman's son brought from the house. We wheeled her into her home and placed her on her bed, which was spotlessly clean. Home at last, she took an offered cigarette from her son and drew deeply.

We said that we needed to return to Tucson. As we left, the daughter turned and took my hand. She made the only direct statement she made to me that day: "I will pray for you forever."

I am left with many questions. How can such despair exist? Not just in Mexico, but anywhere? Why does no one seem to care? What is the value of human life? What was this woman's life for? Or her children's, for that matter?

A part of me says that I should pray for this humble family and those like them. But there's also a part of me which says, "What will that do? Nothing will change. They have prayed as well, and look at their plight."

So, I will pray and hope that my prayers will make a difference.

When I returned home, I prayed that this woman be taken from her pain quickly. She is my relative. The next afternoon, my friend called me to say that the old woman had died during the night.

Metakuye Oyasin.

## CHAPTER 20
# DECISIONS

In the Gospel of St. Luke, when Christ is calling his disciples, there is a description of Simon and his companions standing with empty nets, dejected on the beach, after a long night of fruitless fishing. Christ approaches and tells them to put their boats into the water and to let down their nets. Simon protests, since every ones knows that few fish can be caught during the day. Nevertheless, he follows Jesus' instructions and the catch is almost more than the two boats can hold.

In this gospel, when Simon saw what had happened, he was amazed and fell on his knees before Jesus and said, "Go, Lord, leave me, sinner that I am."

As I read once more what for the fifth Sunday after Epiphany was the gospel lesson for the week, I found that a number of things were taking place. First, Simon and his friends saw a miracle take place. Second, Simon was brought face to face with his failings and shortcomings. Third, at this darkest point, Simon was told that his life would be different from what it had been up to that point.

As I listened to this gospel lesson, I was struck by a parallel with something that takes place at the Sun Dance. Often, there are dancers there who have spent years destroying their lives with drugs and alcohol. By the power of the Great Mystery, they are led into a rehabilitation program designed specifically to address addiction and the spiritual needs of Native Americans. Here, the participants come face to face with their own mortality, with their lost spirituality and they realize that their lives are being wasted. A decision is made to seek the traditional ways.

As spiritually insightful and fulfilling as the Sun Dance is for myself, I can only imagine how these qualities are magnified for these Native American people who have been out of touch with their own spiritual heritage, who have abused body, mind, soul and spirit and who are now about to be reawakened to the power and sacredness of this ceremony. I can only guess what it must be like to stand in the presence of the sacred and to be released from the bonds of self-destruction. It must be overwhelming.

This is where I think about Simon on that long ago beach. I wonder if, like him, there are those standing on the sand before the sacred tree who say: "Leave me, sinner that I am."

And yet, the strong but gentle pull of the voice of the Creator on human hearts is there and no person is likely to refuse, especially when it seems that there is nothing more to lose in life.

## Chapter 21
# Finding the Center

I have witnessed the emotion of Native peoples returning to the sweat lodge ceremony after a long absence. They say that it is like coming home. The ancient connections between each person and the earth, air, water and fire are re-established in the presence of the Creator. These connections have never been broken, only lost.

But what about those of us who are not indigenous? We often don't know who we are, what we are or where we came from. For those of us who can never go "home" again, it is essential that we begin the process of listening to the spirit of the land we now walk upon, the land called Turtle Island. I think it is essential that we begin to listen to these indigenous peoples who have been here for thousands of years. What do they have to say? What can they teach each of us?

Each of us must come from our own perspective in dealing with spirituality. As one raised in the Christian tradition, I find many parallels between scripture and traditional Native beliefs, especially in those areas dealing with the reverence for the Great Mystery and for the land. Look at the stories surrounding John the Baptist and Jesus and their relationship with the sacred and with nature. I find it odd that so much of this essential doctrine has been lost or totally overlooked in Christian churches.

Jesus, his disciples and all of his early followers, lived off the land.

They were intimately connected to God and to the cycles of life. They sought guidance of God and found the spirit of His presence in all things. It was this closeness, this interconnectedness that allowed Jesus and John to open themselves to the words of Yahweh. It was this unity, this total oneness with nature that was so threatening to the urban establishment in Jerusalem. They labeled it was wildness and closed their doors against it.

There is a parallel between Native American beliefs and the story of Jesus Christ. It involves the time of seeking, of going into the desert to meet with the sacred stillness in order to see God and find direction. Christ went into the desert for forty days. In Lakota spiritual tradition, this is called "Hamblecha," the vision quest. It is an essential part of each person's spiritual walk toward the Creator.

Today, few people are willing to accept the suffering involved in seeking a vision. They also have lost the courage to step out of the established norm and seek spiritual guidance on a one-to-one basis. What would happen if each of us who felt led to walk a new and more intense spiritual path were to step forward and seek a oneness with the Creator? What would happen if we returned to the basics of early Christianity, to the "wildness" of a path leading to unity with all of nature and the Great Mystery?

The vision quest or Christ's seeking God's face in the desert can be life altering. The seeker comes, rootless, disconnected, hungry and alone. He leaves in peace, at one with all things. It is within the intersection of place, person, belief and God that the solutions to life can come. It is within this sacred hoop that we can begin to walk in balance and in harmony and find the center.

Metakuye Oyasin

# ABOUT THE AUTHOR

Garth Nielsen was born in Glendale, California, in 1938. He grew up in Nevada and has had a love of the high deserts all his life. Garth has also lived in Oregon, New York, Utah, Colorado, New Mexico and Arizona.

As an adult, he was adopted in  private ceremonies by the Hau-de-no-sau-nee (Iroquois). Garth has been guided throughout his life to embrace and become one with Native American traditional ceremonies. He feels that he has been blessed by being able to participate in these ceremonies and to be able to talk to many traditional elders over the years.

Garth Nielsen has written this book as a way of saying thanks to all those who have reached out their hands in friendship over the years.

Garth is retired and he and his wife, Barbara, currently live in a small community in Northern California.

To contact Garth Nielsen  he has requested you use email as the best form of comunication.

email: garth.barb.nielsen@gmail.com

Sketched Portrait of Garth Nielsen  by Nancy S. Pinadel

Made in the USA
Lexington, KY
13 August 2014